600
21

BRITISH PADDLE STEAMERS

PS *Maid of the Loch* on her native Loch Lomond

BRITISH
PADDLE
STEAMERS

Geoffrey Body
A M Inst T

DAVID & CHARLES : NEWTON ABBOT

ISBN 0 7153 5118 4

COPYRIGHT NOTICE

*Set in Intertype Baskerville
and printed in Great Britain
by Clarke, Doble & Brendon Limited Plymouth
for David & Charles (Publishers) Limited
South Devon House Newton Abbot Devon*

CONTENTS

5

LIST OF ILLUSTRATIONS

9

INTRODUCTION

A L T H O U G H there are many excellent volumes dealing with the paddle steamers of a particular era, area, or type, there is very little material dealing with the subject as a whole. This book attempts to fill that gap by providing a picture of the development of the British paddle steamer in all its major forms, rôles, and spheres of operation. It would, of course, have been quite impossible to refer individually to all the British paddlers or even to all the notable ones because of the sheer numbers involved. Instead, each main aspect of the paddle steamer's history is exemplified by typical or notable vessels with this data amplified at the end of the book.

There is a very natural tendency to think of the paddle steamer primarily as a pleasure cruising vessel. Certainly this was its main rôle in later years and thus the one in which it will be mainly remembered. However, in its history of over 150 years the paddle steamer has participated in all the main forms of shipping activity, from trans-ocean passenger operations with all their prestige and glamour to the vital but mundane towing tasks, and the to-ing and fro-ing of ferry work. And to all of these it has made a worthwhile contribution in terms of public wellbeing.

In many of its rôles the British paddle steamer made more than just a contribution. In its early years it was a major factor in the development of areas such as the Clyde and in the emerging British holiday habit. Many resorts of today owe much to the paddle steamer. Paddle steamers, by offering cheaper and more convenient travel than the stage coaches, stimulated commerce between our coastal towns and between Great Britain and other countries. Before the paddle steamer there was no sort of reliability to the overseas news or mail and importing and exporting were at the mercy of wind and tide. All the early ocean steamers were paddle vessels. They helped to bring down fares and reduce freight rates with beneficial effects upon the trade, and thus the prosperity and wellbeing, of the British people.

After a century of operation, the paddle steamer became mainly a pleasure and excursion vessel. Year after year, all around the British coasts, these immaculate vessels gave hours of healthy enjoyment to the crowds of trippers and holiday-makers. The settings were varied—the beautiful Clyde estuary, down the busy Thames, a visit to Lundy Island—but each steamer gave full value and the crews seemed to enjoy their duty. Tastes change and as more sophisticated pleasures made their appearance in the 1950s and 60s, so the paddlers started to disappear leaving just memories of wheeling gulls, gleaming tea urns, a colourful, immaculate engine room, and the frothy wake from churning paddle wheels.

Soon British paddle steamers will be mainly memories with just a few preserved examples to give the recollections a wistful substance. If this book has a dedication—as opposed to a pur-pose—it is to those who designed, built, manned, and operated our paddle steamers. Whether it be the happy hours of trippers or in the sterner days of war these vessels gave us much and my book seeks, with humility, to acknowledge and record this.

CHAPTER ONE

THE BIRTH OF THE STEAMBOAT

E VIDENCE of vessels driven by paddles and of ideas for such vessels is scattered over the centuries as far back as Roman times. The Romans themselves are known to have had paddle vessels propelled by oxen and there are several references to Chinese manually operated paddle warships. Although the history of the paddle goes back at least as far as the history of steam there could be no beginning to the idea of a paddle steamer until the steam engine had completed the first stages of its development.

The power of steam was known to man as early as the era of ancient Greece when Hero of Alexandria devised several types of steam apparatus. Hero's seventy-eight recorded experiments not only 'took the lid off' some of the trickery of contemporary priesthood but also foreshadowed the turbine engine. For centuries sailing men had blessed the wind with one breath and cursed its absence, direction, or weakness with the next and once the steam engine became a reality it is not surprising that many attempts were soon made to apply it to shipping.

Among the earliest to recognise the possible applications of steam on land and sea was Saloman de Caus (France 1576–1635) but the first real breakthrough came at the end of the seventeenth century when Thomas Savery's water-raising engine of 1698 followed the first cylinder-and-piston engine, by Denis Papin. Included among Papin's many later ideas were thoughts of a paddle boat driven by an atmospheric steam engine but nothing came of this before he died in 1714. In the year of 1705 success came also to Thomas Newcomen who used similar ideas. In his beam engine, the admission of steam into the cylinder lifted a counterpoised beam. The steam was then condensed by a jet of

15

cold water which created a vacuum and the piston reversed its direction as a result of the atmospheric pressure.

Paddle steamer machinery has always been impressive but to have accommodated Newcomen's massive and inefficient engine in a ship would have been too much even for the most imaginative. It was not until the second half of the eighteenth century that any amount of purposeful thought was given to applying steam to ships and this followed the second breakthrough in steam, that of James Watt in 1769. Watt, with his separate condenser, steam jacketing and engine-worked air pump to provide the vacuum in the condenser, heralded the era of a relatively efficient steam engine. In 1782 Watt added to his achievements by patenting the double-acting principle and that of the expansive power of steam.

Before considering in some detail the way the idea of a paddle steamer developed in the second half of the century, mention must be made of the towboat plans patented by Jonathan Hulls of Gloucestershire in 1736. This design was the ancestor of the paddle steamer in this country and provided for a boiler forward and a Newcomen engine amidships driving stern paddles through a system of ropes and pulleys.

From 1770 onwards there were several notable attempts to use steam power to propel ships. In 1774 Comte J. B. d'Auxiron equipped a steamboat with a two-cylinder atmospheric engine but the boat foundered before the trials got under way. One year later Jacques C. Perier operated a small steamboat on the Seine but this did not have sufficient power to stem the current.

Next on the scene was the Marquis Claude de Jouffroy d'Abbans. In June 1778 he tried out a curious vessel on the Doubs river. It was a 43ft boat equipped with two Newcomen engines which operated two flat paddles rather like ducks' feet. Nothing really functioned as d'Abbans had hoped and it was not until 1783 that he achieved real success. This was at Ecully, near Lyons, with a wooden vessel called *Pyroscaphe* equipped with an engine of the horizontal, double-acting cylinder type and driving side paddle wheels through a set of ratchets. On 15 July *Pyroscaphe* performed a fifteen-minute run against the Seine current but her boiler was the real weakness and proved incapable of meeting the demands of the engine for steam.

The next round of development took place in America where John Fitch produced his first steamboat model in 1785. Subsequently he promoted a company which produced a boat 45ft long and with six overhead-supported paddles on each side. This performed fairly successfully on the Delaware river in August 1787, achieving a speed of three miles per hour. The next improvement was a stern wheeler 60ft long and 12ft wide named *Experiment* which started operating a public service in 1790. This failed to make money and had to be abandoned. At this time several other Americans were working on the idea of a steamboat. Samuel Morey undertook a number of experiments between 1790 and 1792 and in 1797 he produced a workable vessel, but his backers ran into financial difficulties.

The scene now switches to Scotland and to a curious partnership between a banker and an engineer. Patrick Miller of Edinburgh was 'a banker of active and ingenious mind who, having realised a fortune by banking, used it as a means of enabling him to work out schemes for the benefit of the public'. From designing paddle boats driven by men and horses he progressed to a twin-hull boat, installing an engine in one hull and the boiler in the other. The engine was made by William Symington who had been working on a steam carriage, the plans for which he patented in 1787. The engine had two vertical atmospheric cylinders of 4in diameter and 18in stroke which operated two chain-driven paddle wheels lying in tandem between the hulls. The vessel, which was 25ft long and 7ft wide, underwent its trials on 14 November 1788 on Dalswinton Loch near Dumfries. The crew consisted of Miller, Symington, Taylor, tutor to Miller's sons and a friend of Symington, Alexander Nasmyth, and Robert Burns. It is recorded 'in the presence of hundreds of spectators who lined the banks of the canal, the boat glided along propelled at the rate of five miles an hour'.

B

In the following year Miller engaged Symington to build a second vessel to his design and the work was carried out by the Carron Iron Company. The floats gave way during the first trial but the vessel performed quite competently on the Forth & Clyde Canal during its second outing. The engine of this second vessel was Symington's adaptation of the Newcomen system with a separate condenser of the Watt type and a complicated transmission of chains and ratchets. It had cylinders of 18in stroke like the first vessel. Miller considered the machinery clumsy and unreliable, as it probably was, and this led to the partners drifting apart. Miller tried to interest James Watt in his project in 1790 and was rebuffed. As a result he turned his mind to other matters.

Here the matter rested until the turn of the century when the project was revived by Thomas, Lord Dundas of Kerse, a governor of the Forth & Clyde Canal. Symington had not worked on steamers since his break with Miller but with the backing of Lord Dundas he arranged for William Hart to build a wooden vessel 56ft long, 18ft wide, and with a depth of 8ft. The vessel had a double stern and rudders and a single paddle wheel was housed in a covered stern recess. The boiler was located to starboard and a 10nhp engine to port. In this new engine Symington forsook the Newcomen principles and provided for a double-acting cylinder of 22in diameter and 4ft stroke with the piston rod guided in slides and the connecting rod acting direct to a crank on the paddle wheel.

The new vessel was very much larger than Symington's previous excursions into the realms of steamboats. She was named *Charlotte Dundas* and in the March of 1802 was put to the test on the Forth & Clyde Canal. Here she promptly proved her worth by towing two laden 70ton sloops for nineteen and a half miles from the wharf at Lock 20 to Port Dundas. Despite a strong wind this journey was accomplished in six hours. Further successful trials took place, but the vessel was not put to regular use because the proprietors feared the effect of her wash on the banks of their canal. Eventually this pioneer was beached in a creek and left to rot. In the meantime Symington had been introduced to the Duke of Bridgewater and had persuaded him to order eight tugs for his canal. Unfortunately the Duke died before the order could be executed and Symington's hopes for the further development of his ideas died with him.

Two more names were destined to figure prominently in the story of the early development of the paddle steamer. These were the names of the American Robert Fulton and of the Scot, Henry Bell. The former, who was experimenting on the River Seine as early as the 1790s, was familiar with the efforts of his contemporaries and his eventual success owes much to the work of other people. Fulton knew both the Duke of Bridgewater and James Watt and is said to have been given a four-mile trip in *Charlotte Dundas* in 1802. Prior to this, Fulton had offered in 1801 to convey Napoleon's troops across the Channel 'on rafts propelled by steam' and for this would hardly have deserved a generous reception in Great Britain. In 1803 Fulton put a boat on the Seine but this broke in two when the machinery was installed.

Success came to Fulton in August 1807 when his paddle steamer *Clermont* or *North River* achieved an upstream journey of 150 miles from New York to Albany. This voyage is especially memorable because *Clermont* was not a small boat but a large vessel 149ft long. The wooden hull was built by Charles Brown of New York, while her 20hp engine was a Boulton & Watt export. It had a vertical cylinder 24in by 4ft driving two 15ft side paddles through hull cranks. *Clermont* encountered prejudice and suspicion as well as enthusiasm and the masters of some sailing ships were instructed to try to collide with her. However, she survived all this and after being rebuilt in 1808 was followed by a line of paddlers on the Hudson river and by the first steam warship *Fulton the First*. This was, in fact, an armoured floating battery with paddle wheels, launched in 1812 for the defence of New York in the 1812–14 Anglo-American war. The vessel was later renamed *Demologos*.

Fulton's efforts prompted the versatile Colonel John Stevens to build and engine the paddle steamer *Phoenix* and to take her out of the Hudson river via the open sea to Philadelphia between 10 and 23 June 1808. *Phoenix*, 101ft long with a beam of 16ft and a draught of 6·75ft, started life with a cross-head engine having two cylinders of 16in diameter and 3ft stroke. Before his efforts with *Phoenix*, Colonel Stevens had done a great deal of experimental work with screw-driven vessels and with tubular boilers.

A contributor to Fulton's success, and a major figure in the development of steamboats, was Henry Bell of Helensburgh. Bell, who was born in Linlithgow on 7 April 1767, had worked in London under Rennie and in 1790 became a chief partner in a Glasgow building firm. Whether it was the numerous wherry-built flyboats which Bell must have seen in Glasgow which prompted his interest in ships is not known. What is known, however, is that Bell was interested in the subject well before the turn of the century.

In 1800 Bell became friendly with a gentleman who owned a small pleasure vessel and agreed with him to instal a 4hp engine in it. This was done but many problems were encountered and even James Watt could not help in solving them. Despite this, Bell was convinced of 'the practicability and great utility of applying steam to the propelling of vessels' and laid a scheme so prefaced before Lord Melville and the Lords of the Admiralty. Unfortunately Nelson alone saw the merit of the new ideas and the scheme was rejected as having 'no value'. It was during this period that Bell corresponded with Fulton and his ideas may well have contributed to the success of *Clermont*. Four years after *Clermont*'s pioneer voyage Bell decided to try once more and placed an order with John Wood of Glasgow for a 24·5ton vessel. This was the *Comet*, destined to be the forerunner of vast numbers of paddle steamers on the Clyde, as the Glasgow to Greenock service which Bell advertised was to be the first step in the development of the watering places of that area.

Comet, which derived its name from the appearance of a comet visible in north-west Scotland in the year of its completion, started regular sailings in August 1812, leaving Broomielaw about noon on Tuesdays, Thursdays, and Saturdays and returning on Mondays, Wednesdays, and Fridays. A fare of four shillings was charged for the best cabin and three shillings for the second-class accommodation. From 2 September 1812 *Comet* started sailing via Tarbert and the Crinan Canal to Oban, Port Appin, and Fort William. Later she was transferred to Grangemouth but returned to the Clyde in August 1819. Just over one year later, on 13 December 1820, *Comet* was making the passage between Fort William and Glasgow when she was driven ashore and wrecked at Doris Mhor outside Crinan. A combination of a strong tide and an east wind had brought about the sad end of this historic vessel but Bell, who was on board at the time, escaped to the shore from the bow along with the other passengers and crew.

Comet was 43·5ft long by 11·25ft by 5·6ft. A square auxiliary sail was stayed to the 25ft smokestack which rose high from the single deck. Originally two paddle wheels were fitted on either side but these were later replaced by single wheels and the vessel lengthed by 22ft. Bell obtained *Comet*'s first engine from John Robertson of Glasgow. It was a small side-lever engine of about 3hp with a cylinder of 11in diameter and 16in stroke. The boiler, externally fired, was of the horizontal type and was purchased from David Napier for £52. Bell agreed to pay £165 for the engine despite Robertson's warning that it would probably be too small for its task. This proved to be the case and after using the engine for two months Bell arranged for Robertson to supply a new 4hp, double-acting, jet condensing engine in its place. This had a single upright cylinder of 12·5in diameter and 16in stroke driving a pair of half side levers by means of two rods. A new price of £365 was agreed to cover both engines and the alterations to the paddle wheels. After these alterations, *Comet* showed herself capable of a speed of five knots.

Although she started a new era in Clyde shipping *Comet* was not a financial success and neither Wood nor Robertson got paid. The vessel's engines were, in fact, salvaged by Bell's unpaid coachbuilder and Bell, in his declining years, was supported by an annuity from the Clyde trustees. Despite the lack of financial rewards neither Wood nor Robertson was daunted, the former building and launching the *Clyde* in 1813 and the latter fitting an engine to *Tay* which was built for him at Dundee in the same year. And so paddle steamers made their debut.

CHAPTER TWO

THE PADDLE STEAMER DEVELOPS

DURING the years between the first voyages of the *Comet* and the early 1820s the paddle steamer had made sufficient impression on the shipping world to ensure its future. Admittedly, many contemporary qualifications would have been made of this statement, but in retrospect there can be little doubt of its truth. Many who accepted the arrival of the paddle steamer saw it as functioning solely on rivers and in sheltered esturial waters, but by 1820 this limited outlook had already been shaken by events. The early developments certainly took place in the estuaries, especially the Clyde, but steamboat owners were soon looking for new spheres in which to try their vessels. An especially notable vessel in this category was the *Margery* or *Marjory*, the first steam packet on the Thames and the first steam vessel to cross to France. This little wooden paddler was very similar to the *Comet*. 63ft long, 12ft wide, and with a draught of 5·5ft, she was built by Archibald MacLachlan & Co for Glasgow merchants. *Margery* was fitted with a 10nhp side-lever engine by James Cook of Tradeston. This had one vertical cylinder of 22in diameter and 2ft stroke and took steam at 2psi pressure from a flat-sided iron boiler. Paddles 8·75ft in diameter with six floats and turning at thirty-two revolutions per minute gave *Margery* a speed of about seven knots.

After operating on the Clyde until November 1814 *Margery* was sold to London owners and commenced a London to Gravesend service on 23 January 1815. *Margery*'s career on the Thames was cut short by the opposition of the Thames watermen who would not allow her free access to the piers. Partly as a result of this she was disposed of to a Paris company and sailed from

Newhaven for Havre on 17 March 1816. In France she became the *Elise* and worked on the Seine, but she did not prove a financial success. Later in 1816, on 9 June, *Defiance*, built by John Wood & Co for William Wager, sailed from Margate to Veere. *Defiance* was 58·1ft long and had a beam of 17·2ft. She boasted an exceptionally tall funnel.

In April 1817 James Watt Jr purchased the 102ton *Caledonia* which had been launched two years earlier and fitted her with new machinery, boilers, and paddle wheels. She was a vessel 94ft long with a beam of 27·67ft and a draught of 9ft. Above decks she had her mast forward and her funnel astern of the paddles with a deck awning rigged abaft the funnel. Below decks her two engines operated paddle-shaft cranks set ninety degrees apart with the 23in by 30in cylinders driving 13ft paddles. On 15 October 1817 *Caledonia* crossed from Margate to Rotterdam and then sailed up the Rhine. On her return she was used for a number of experiments before being sold to become the first Danish steamboat.

Once the ice had been broken, the advantages offered by a steamer over the sailing packets which were entirely at the mercy of the winds began gradually to be realised. William Denny's famous shipyard at Dumbarton led the way with the first steamer to be designed for the open sea and all the weathers it could provide. Engined by David Napier, this was *Rob Roy*, a privately owned vessel which, in 1821, had the distinction of starting the first cross-channel service in the world. After two years in the Glasgow–Belfast trade the 90ton, 30hp *Rob Roy* was transferred to the Dover–Calais run. There she so impressed the French government that she was purchased to carry the English mails. New ownership brought a change of name, first to *Henri Quatre* and later to *Duc d'Orleans*.

Rob Roy was the brainchild of David Napier. Napier's father owned a foundry at Dumbarton using two steam engines to bore the cannons which he made there. David was born after the business moved to Glasgow, and grew up in an atmosphere of machinery and of its practical applications. As a boy he marvelled at the *Charlotte Dundas* and when he took over the business on the death of his father in 1813, the twenty-year-old David soon turned his thoughts to making marine engines. At the time popular opinion considered that it was impossible to construct engines powerful enough to withstand the strains arising in heavy seas. Young Napier thought otherwise and, after erecting a new works at Camlachie, he started a detailed study of hull design and fluid resistance. Influenced considerably by French studies of the latter, Napier eventually produced the design of a vessel with a radically fined prow and hull. The model was taken to Dennys with instructions to build a lifesize version. The result was *Rob Roy* whose 80ft length and 16ft beam measurements were more suggestive of the American clipper building ratios than of the traditional four to one of the East Indiamen. As we have seen, *Rob Roy* was a great success when she started to sail from Greenock in 1818. This encouraged Napier to improve his designs and in 1819 *Talbot* and *Ivanhoe* were launched. These vessels each had two 30hp Napier engines and set the seal of practicability on the use of paddle steamers on the open seas. Of 120tons, *Talbot* had the distinction of becoming the first mail steamer between Holyhead and Dublin.

Meanwhile, events had moved fast in the sphere of esturial waters. In areas like the Clyde, where ships had always played a big part in communications, the advantages of the paddle steamer, especially its manoeuvrability, led to rapid development. The *Comet* had been followed by the steamers *Elizabeth* and *Clyde* and after these two came *Glasgow* in 1813. In 1814 came the first signs of a boom, with nine steamers being added to the Clyde fleet. One of these was *Industry* which was not only the Clyde's seventh steamer but was destined to become the oldest steamer in the world before being broken up. The following year, 1815, *Dumbarton Castle* started work on the Rothesay run and services were also extended from Dunoon to Inverary.

Between 1815 and 1819 a total of twenty-six vessels appeared on the Clyde waters while in the 1820s thirty-two steamers were built, the greater number of them by James Lang and William

Denny of Dumbarton. These vessels played a major part in the expansion of the Clyde watering places by providing regular services from Glasgow to Dumbarton, Greenock, Loch Fyne, Inverness, Largs, Millport, Gareloch, Loch Goil, Helensburgh, Ayr, Rothesay, and Kilmun. By 1822 Fort William, Tobermory, and Skye were being served by the Glasgow paddle steamer *Highlander*. All the Clyde steamers of this period were of wood, most of them about 100ft long and powered by a side-lever engine.

John Robertson of Glasgow, maker of the *Comet*'s engine, used the experience to build another engine and the *Clyde* was ordered to fit this rather than the other way round. She was built in 1813 and was 72ft long, had a beam of 14ft and a draught of 7·5ft. In the June of 1813 she started to work between Glasgow, Greenock, and Gourock and took three and a half hours to complete the forty-eight-mile round trip. In 1823 she was renamed *Gourock*, in 1825 *Lord Byron*, in 1826 *George IV*, and was finally scrapped in 1828.

The year after *Clyde* started work Robertson fitted a further engine to the *Tay* which he had built for him at Dundee and which ran for four years between Dundee and Perth before transferring to the Glasgow to Lochgoilhead run as the *Oscar*. Robertson had two more vessels built at Dundee, the *Caledonia* and the *Humber*. Both of these went south to work from Hull to Selby and from Hull to Gainsborough. Further paddle steamers followed in 1817 and 1818 but by now the competition on the Clyde had grown quite fierce and it brought about Robertson's ruin.

Not only did the *Clyde* have an interesting career, but so did her contemporary *Elizabeth*. This early pioneer had the distinction of being the first vessel to enter the Mersey when Colin Watson brought her from the Clyde to work between Liverpool and Runcorn. She was not a financial success and was sold in the following year to be succeeded by such vessels as the *Earl of Bridgewater* whose boiler burst in 1824.

The distinction of being the first steamer on the Mersey is also claimed for a vessel called *Henry Bell*. It is known that a vessel of this name was operating on the Liverpool to Glasgow route and calling at Manx ports in 1823 but the claim to be Liverpool's first steamer rests on an article in the *Manx Advertiser* of the same period and may be somewhat suspect. All that is known with certainty is that on 30 June 1815 the *Liverpool Mercury* recorded :

> On Wednesday last, at about noon, the public curiosity was considerably excited by the arrival of the first steamer ever seen in our river. She came from the Clyde, and in her passage called at Ramsey, in the Isle of Man, which place she left early on the same morning. We believe she is intended to ply between this port and Runcorn, or even occasionally as far as Warrington. Her cabin will contain about one hundred passengers.

The year 1816 was very much a year of steamboat expansion on Merseyside with vessels such as the locally built *Duke of Wellington* appearing on the Ellesmere Port ferry. Other 1816 vessels were *Prince Regent*, which sank in a storm near Ellesmere Port six years later, and *Princess Charlotte*, the first steamer on the ferry to Eastham. Connecting with the Chester and Shrewsbury coaches, this ferry was followed by the establishment of a Liverpool to Tranmere service.

The Dumbarton-built steam packet *Greenock* arrived in the waters of the Irish Sea in 1816. The first record of this vessel is a statement in the *Newsletter* of 23 April 1816 to the effect that she would be operating daily between Belfast, Carrickfergus, and Bangor. Next, a Manx newspaper records that 'great curiosity was exhibited at Douglas by the arrival of the steam packet *Greenock* on the passage to Liverpool'. This was on 7 May 1816, the *Greenock* making a short trip to Laxey before continuing her voyage to Liverpool where she was to operate under the name *Countess of Bridgewater*. Also in the year 1816 a steamer is recorded as being in use at Liverpool for towing sailing vessels out to sea, *Hibernia* started a packet service between Howth and Holyhead, and the paddle steamers *Waterloo* and *Belfast* began alternate day sailings between Liverpool and Dublin.

During the early years the Clyde was an exporting area for paddle steamers. Its shipbuilders had pioneered the new vessel and earned a lead in time and experience while at the same time the general haste to get rich from providing steamer services resulted in over-provision and a consequent surplus of vessels. One of the results of this situation was that in the other major estuaries the mixture of locally-built steamers and Clyde imports produced a highly cosmopolitan fleet. This was especially the case in the Mersey estuary where steamers were needed for a wider variety of work than in most other areas and which was easily reached from Glasgow.

As a consequence of these influences, the Mersey in the 1820s was a colourful part of the paddle vessel scene. Its vessels varied from ferries to tugs and bore a wide variety of names, some earthy, some perpetuating the romance of the Clyde, and others, like the *Lady Stanley* of 1821, honouring local people. As in other places, vessel design embraced both the conventional trend and the search for new layout and hull forms. The latter is illustrated by the 1817 ferry *Etna,* one of the first vessels in regular service to have a double hull with the paddles located centrally.

London's shipping community first became seriously interested in steamships in 1814, two years after *Comet*'s debut and one year before Waterloo. This interest led to the *Margery*'s journey south via the Forth & Clyde Canal and to the 14hp, Cook-built, *Thames* making a similar journey but by way of Dublin and Land's End. This vessel was 79ft long, 16ft wide, and of 70 gross tons. She had a very tall funnel which did duty as a mast and twice during the journey south boats put out from the shore to come to her aid, thinking that the steamer was on fire. Built in 1813 as *Argyle,* she was followed in 1816 by two further vessels so that by the end of that year, although *Margery* had left for France, three vessels (including the tug *Majestic*) were in steam on London's river with services as far afield as Margate. The three vessels had engines of 12, 14, and 16hp while steamers of 12hp and of 6hp were under construction.

In 1817 three vessels were registered including *Favourite* of

160tons burden and the 70ton *London*. The former replaced a vessel destroyed by fire and was fitted with a 40nhp engine by Boulton & Watt of Soho. She did excursion work to Margate. *London* was built by Searle of Westminster and was fitted with a single-cylinder, grasshopper type of engine with narrow boilers each side, supplied by Butterley & Co and producing a speed of 14knots. She was 85ft long with a beam of 14ft and worked first between Richmond and London but met with considerable opposition from the Thames watermen who tried to get her banned. She later worked from Gravesend to Southend.

Six steamers were registered in London in 1818, seven in 1819, and nine in 1820. Thereafter the number of vessels reached and maintained double figures until in 1830 there were fifty-seven vessels registered of which forty-two were actually operating on the Thames. The remainder were either laid up or employed at other ports. One of the 1818 vessels was the 160ton *Victory* which was built at Rotherhithe for a Richmond–Gravesend–Margate service. After losing money initially, *Victory* started to pay her way as an excursion steamer until she collided with a brig off Barking in 1842. Another 1818 paddle steamer was the *London Engineer* which had a double paddle wheel located within the hull and driven by two-cylinder Maudslay Sons & Field engines of 70hp. The main deck of *London Engineer* was simple with circulating areas fore and aft and a slightly raised steering position forward of the tall funnel. Below, the hard seats and cramped conditions forward contrasted with the spacious saloon aft of the three furnaces.

Among the London vessels launched in 1820 was one of special note. This was the wooden paddler *Eagle* which was built at Deptford. She was bought by a timber merchant, Thomas Brockle-bank, and proved so successful in the business of carrying Thames passengers that other businessmen joined the venture and the General Steam Navigation company was born. Another notable GSN vessel which followed *Eagle* was the 1826 *Magnet*, a Lime-house-built vessel. She was of 296tons gross, had dimensions of 139·1ft by 21·2ft by 7·5ft and was powered by a 150nph engine.

Her work was in the Channel and on London to Ramsgate excursions.

The 158ft *Ramona* built at Rotherhithe in 1828 worked between London and Rotterdam and in 1842 went to Yarmouth on coasting work. There was also *Columbine* which was built at Deptford in 1826 and was of 393tons and 140hp. She worked first between Richmond and Margate and then between Custom House and Ramsgate with occasional excursions to Boulogne. She was stranded near Rotterdam in 1855.

In addition to the Clyde the other Scottish estuaries were the scenes of paddle steamer development. In 1814 the 12hp *Stirling* began to ply between Stirling and Leith and in the following year two other vessels were added on the Forth and one on the Tay, operating between Perth and Dundee. By 1822, *James Watt*, the first steamer registered at Lloyds, was working between London and Leith and in 1825 the Clyde steamer *Marquis of Bute* took up station at Belfast as *Bangor Castle* and worked for the next three years between Belfast and Bangor with occasional excursions to Donaghadee. There was a steamer on the Avon working between Bristol and Bath as early as 1813 while a Leeds-built vessel appears to have been in use between Norwich and Yarmouth at about the same period. By 1816 there were steamboats on the Trent, the Tyne, the Ouse, the Humber, the Orwell, and the Thames. July 1820 saw the first steamer in Southampton Water, with *Prince Coburg* and *Thames* following in 1821.

By the early 1820s most of the main resorts, ports, and estuaries had paddle steamers at work providing ferry and other local services, a variety of excursions and some longer distance voyages. The path of development from a curious novelty to a useful part of the national transport facilities had not been an easy one. Many people were apprehensive about travelling in these early vessels and the number of mishaps did nothing to reassure them. Some attempt had been made at regulation including an 1824 Thames speed limit of 'three knots with the tide and four against it'. Steamboat operators had to contend with many difficulties including the prophets of doom contending that exhaust smoke would poison the passengers and the more mundane problem of finding and training engineers.

Antagonism to the new steamers was particularly marked on the Thames where Captain Cortis of the *Margery* was prosecuted and removed from his command because he was not a freeman of the Watermen's Company which had the sole rights to carry passengers on the river. Later steamers found themselves delayed by the watermen's tactics of rowing across their bows to slow them down. But the steamers were much more comfortable and with publicity for the library, backgammon, and other amusements provided on board, patronage steadily developed until 50,000 people were travelling to Margate by water by 1825 and the total number of passengers on the Thames was soon to rise to over one million each year. The paddle steamer was here to stay.

CHAPTER THREE

OCEAN PIONEERS

PRIOR to the advent of the steam engine the design of British merchant vessels had remained largely unaltered for many years. On the routes to the east the East India Company enjoyed a monopoly position and there was no real incentive to build better ships. For nearly two hundred years a period of stagnation existed with the average size of British ships rising by only twenty tons during the whole of the seventeenth and eighteenth centuries. During this period the Americans began to build, good, cheap, softwood vessels with continuous increases in size and improvements in design. The result was that by the beginning of the nineteenth century it could truthfully be said that the Americans were the masters of the transatlantic commerce. A Black Ball sailing vessel left New York for Liverpool on the first and fifteenth days of each month, with a Swallowtail departure on the eighth and a Red Star pacemaker sailing on the twenty-fourth. The journey times were fast too, *Caledonia* achieving 15days 22hours on the westward crossing and *Columbia* 15days 18hours.

With the constant challenge from the New World, with steam engine designs steadily improving, and the British paddle steamers forsaking the estuaries for the open seas, the challenge of the Atlantic became an increasingly attractive lure to British shipping interests. At this period the rate of steamboat development was such that by 1825 forty-five steamship companies were registered in London alone. Nevertheless, the honour of being the first paddle steamer to cross the Atlantic goes to an American vessel, the auxiliary paddle steamer *Savannah* which sailed for Liverpool on 24 May 1819. *Savannah*, a carvel-built vessel of 320tons by Francis Fickett of New York, was launched on 22

Page 33: (above) A lithograph reproduction of *Charlotte Dundas*, the pioneer towing vessel built by William Symington; (below) the pioneer passenger paddle steamer *Comet* was originally built with double paddle wheels as shown by this model

Page 34: *(above)* After working on the Thames as the *Margery*, this vessel became the first paddle steamer to cross to France where she became the *Elise*; *(below)* the Clyde veteran PS *Industry*, destined to become the oldest steamer in the world before being broken up

August 1818. Some 110ft long and 25·8ft beam, *Savannah* had
been intended as a sail packet and carried a full rig. The auxiliary
steam engines, 15·25ft paddles and elbow swivel funnel were
something of an afterthought. Stephen Vail of the Speedwell
Iron Works, New Jersey provided the 90ihp engine. This
was fed with steam at 2psi and had a single cylinder of 40in
diameter and 5ft stroke inclined to act directly on the paddle
shaft.

Savannah used her collapsible paddle wheels to assist her east-
ward crossing of the Atlantic but, after being hawked around
Europe in search of a purchaser, she eventually returned to
Savannah under canvas. Until she was wrecked in 1821 she
passed her days as a coastwise sail packet and thus the honour
of the first westward crossing of the Atlantic went to a British
vessel. The 428ton PS *Rising Star* was ordered in 1818 by
Thomas Cochrane as a steam warship for use in the revolution
in Chile. Two years passed before the builder, Daniel Brent of
Rotherhithe, got round to laying down the keel and the *Rising
Star* was eventually launched in February 1821. She was fitted
with twin-cylinder engines of some 70nhp operating two paddle
wheels located within the hull and on either side of the centre
keel. *Rising Star* sailed from Gravesend for Valparaiso in October
1821. Both sail and steam were used on the journey which took
six months to complete owing to the need to repair a leak en
route. After a short trading career this pioneer was wrecked in
1830.

Various other pioneers followed but these early Atlantic crossings were all by sailing vessels which used their paddles only
when the winds were contrary or non-existent. There were two
main obstacles to further development. One was the amount of
fuel needed to feed the early, inefficient boilers. The other was
the effect of sea water on their iron plates. The sea water caused
the boilers to scale up with the result that the engines had to be
stopped every few days while the boilers were blown out. Boilers
and furnaces slowly improved in efficiency while the second problem rapidly disappeared after 1834 when Samuel Hall patented

C

a practical surface condenser which enabled boilers to be fed with fresh distilled water and so keep in constant operation.

It was a British vessel which was first to cross the Atlantic under continuous steam power. She was the *Sirius*, a small wooden paddler built at Leith in 1837 by Robert Menzies & Son. And she achieved this honour almost accidentally. The American Julius Smith and MacGregor Laird, brother of John Laird of Birkenhead and a pioneer Liverpool shipowner, had just formed the British & American Steam Navigation Company. They had ordered the paddle steamer *British Queen* for the opening of their new Atlantic service in April 1838 but her engines were not ready in time and *Sirius* was chartered instead. Thus it transpired that instead of a quiet run between London and Cork for the St George Steam Packet Company *Sirius* found herself sailing from Cork Harbour in a thrilling battle with the Atlantic and with a much larger steamship.

Sirius had 320nhp side-lever engines made by Thomas Wingate & Co of Whiteinch near Glasgow and equipped with two cylinders of 60in diameter and 6ft stroke. These drove 24ft paddle wheels, each with twelve fixed radial floats about 8·5ft long and turning at 15rpm to produce a speed of about nine knots. Thanks to Hall's condensers the vessel's rectangular flue boilers remained in constant operation supplying steam at 5psi and consuming 24tons of coal daily in the process.

On 1 March 1838 British newspapers carried the notable announcement

> The three-masted, topsail schooner *Sirius* equipped with auxiliary steam-driven paddle wheels, a most graceful and elegant vessel owned by the British & American Steam Navigation Coy, will sail for New York on April 4 and commence the return journey on May 1.

Forty passengers responded, eleven travelling in the main cabins, eight in the forward cabins and twenty-one in the steerage accommodation. Little did they know that they were to participate in the first of many steam races across the Atlantic and that before their stormy trip was over the little vessel would not only have burned her 453 tons of coal and 43 barrels of resin but would also have been forced to feed woodwork and spars to the furnaces in order to keep them alight.

Sirius duly sailed from London with a crew of thirty-five under Lieutenant R. Roberts RN and, after taking coal at Cork, left that port on 4 April 1838. Just four days later the 1,320ton PS *Great Western* was scheduled to leave Bristol and although bad weather delayed her sailing until the following day, the same bad weather was giving *Sirius* a rough time as she battled her way out into the mid-Atlantic. Now the race was on with *Sirius* never exceeding a daily run of 136 miles in her first week out, while *Great Western* averaged 200 miles daily. The best the smaller vessel could manage was an average speed of 6·7knots whereas *Great Western*'s 450nhp engines supplied by Maudslay, Sons & Field were producing some two knots more than this.

At first the gap between the two vessels narrowed rapidly but as *Sirius* burned more of her coal and got lighter she began to equal the performance of her rival. On one day she ran 218 miles which compared with her performance of only 89 miles on the second day of the voyage. Then, on 22 April, after eighteen days and ten hours sailing, *Sirius* arrived safely off New York and the exciting and historic race was over. Early the following day *Great Western* arrived and was also mightily acclaimed. She too had achieved a triumph by completing the journey in fifteen days and five hours.

Great Western was one of the many ventures of Isambard Kingdom Brunel of Great Western Railway fame. She was 236ft long, of 35·3ft beam, and 58·3ft over her paddle boxes, and had been built at Bristol to Brunel's designs by William Patterson. After her epic first journey across the Atlantic she continued to ply between New York and Bristol until 1846, crossing that ocean sixty-four times altogether. She was then sold to the Royal Mail Steam Packet Company Limited for service between Southampton and the West Indies and was finally broken up at Vauxhall in 1857. *Sirius*, which was only 178·4ft long and of 703tons gross register, returned to Falmouth and London in the May of 1838 and after a second crossing in the July, settled down to a less adventurous life in home waters. She lasted until January 1847 when, while on a voyage between Glasgow and Cork, she ran onto a reef in Ballycotton Bay and became a total wreck.

In addition to the British & American Steam Navigation Company and the Great Western Steamship Company, a third company now sought a share of the transatlantic business. The Transatlantic Steamship Company, like the British & American, went to the Irish trade for its first steamer, chartering the 617ton *Royal William* from the City of Dublin Steam Packet Company. Built of wood by William and Thomas Wilson of Liverpool in 1837, *Royal William* had two masts, barquetine-rigged and was 200ft long. She was powered by 270nhp side-lever engines by Fawcett & Preston of Liverpool and these drew steam at 5psi from boilers fired by a mixture of coal and compressed peat. *Royal William* made her first Atlantic crossing just over seven years after her 450ton Canadian namesake had crossed from west to east using both sail and steam. She left Liverpool on 5 July 1838 with thirty-two passengers and ten thousand letters and arrived at New York eighteen days and twenty-three hours later having achieved an average speed of 7·3knots and the distinction of being the smallest steamer ever to cross the Atlantic.

After three more crossings *Royal William* returned in 1839 to more humdrum work with her original owners. Like so many other noble ships she ultimately became a coal hulk being finally scrapped just fifty years after her first Atlantic venture. Her retirement from the deep-sea shipping lanes was due to the advent of *Liverpool*, a grand two-funnel vessel which had been built by Humble & Milcrest of Liverpool for Sir John Tobin, but which the Transatlantic company had purchased before completion. The three-masted *Liverpool* was of 1,150 gross tons and was stoutly built of oak and elm with pine planking. She had two large saloons and cabins fitted with ninety-eight berths. *Liverpool*'s 468nhp side-lever engines came from G. Forrester & Co of Liverpool and drove 28·5ft diameter paddle wheels at 15rpm.

The two cylinders were of 75in diameter and 7ft stroke and were fed with steam at 5psi from four rectangular boilers.

Liverpool, the first two-funnel vessel on the Atlantic route, sailed from the port of Liverpool on 20 October 1838 but her sixty passengers did not reach New York until 23 November. A violent storm forced the vessel back into Cork until 6 November. When the voyage again got under way it occupied sixteen days and seventeen hours during which *Liverpool* consumed 465tons of coal to obtain a mean speed of 7·9knots. Although her run had not been as fast as that of the *Great Western*, *Liverpool* had shown what steam could achieve and such journeys continued to make impressive comparison with the relative unpredictability of the sailing ships on the route. It is recorded that when the Canadian Joseph Howe was becalmed on the *Tyrian* he was so impressed with a visit to the passing *Sirius* that his influence later helped to persuade the Admiralty to offer a steam packet contract between England and the New World. Before the Transatlantic Steamship Company was wound up in July 1840, *Liverpool* had made seven trips across the Atlantic. All had made a loss. The vessel passed to the Peninsular & Oriental Steam Navigation Company Limited and was wrecked off Cape Finisterre in 1846.

Two more vessels remain to be mentioned as playing a major part in the first chapter of the Atlantic story. They are the PS *British Queen* and PS *President*. Both belonged to the British & American Steam Navigation Company.

The three-masted, barque-rigged *British Queen* was not only the largest vessel afloat at the time of her launch but was also an extremely handsome ship and the pride of her builders, Curling & Young of Limehouse. She was 275ft long and of 1,862tons gross with accommodation which included a dining saloon 60ft long and 207 berths, 103 forward and the remainder aft. As the bow figurehead she boasted a splendid gleaming white representation of Queen Victoria. *British Queen* first sailed from London on 10 July 1839 and called at Portsmouth before heading for the open sea. She left Portsmouth on 12 July carrying 600tons of coal, and her 500nph engines and 30ft paddles brought her to New York by 27 July. After completing the crossing eight more times *British Queen* was sold to the Belgian Government for an Antwerp–Cowes–New York service. She did not prove economic and was broken up in 1842.

The successor to *British Queen* was the ill-fated *President*. From the same builders, *President* at 268ft long was slightly the shorter of the two but she was broader and stood at 2,360tons gross register. Schooner rigged and with three masts, she was solidly built of oak and had three decks, the upper one flush from stem to stern. On her maiden voyage from Liverpool on 1 August 1840 there was no hint of the tragedy to come and *President* achieved a trip of sixteen and a half days at a mean speed of 8·4knots. On her second return trip from New York she was under the command of Lieutenant R. Roberts RN of *Sirius* fame. A hundred and thirty-six people embarked, many no doubt thrilled at the prospect of the steamer voyage in front of them and none suspecting that they would not be seen or heard of again. For this is, in fact, just what did happen. After her departure on 11 March 1841 *President* just disappeared. She is known to have encountered a severe Atlantic gale and she may have been let down by her machinery which was reputed to be sound but under-powered. She had 540nhp side-lever engines by Fawcett & Preston of Liverpool. These used steam at 5psi from rectangular flue boilers to drive the 31ft diameter paddle wheels at the usual 15rpm.

Not unnaturally attention tended to be focused on the Atlantic seaway. Not only did it provide all the challenge necessary for a steamship but in addition there was the natural desire to assail the American commercial position. Nevertheless, steamers were making a name for themselves on other routes. Perhaps the best known of these was the auxiliary paddle steamer *Enterprise* which won fame by being the first steamer to pass round the Cape to India.

From about 1819 onwards officials concerned with the government of India had been trying to encourage the development of light draught steamers as an aid to communications and control. As part of this campaign the 'Steam Committee' of Calcutta offered a prize of £8,000 for any steam vessel capable of making the voyage out from England in seventy days. This induced Henry Johnston, a naval officer, to sail back from Calcutta to England to try to arrange for a vessel in which to attempt the prize. The result was the diminutive wooden steamer *Enterprise* built by Gordon & Co of Deptford in 1825. At 122ft long she was even smaller than *Sirius*. She was 27ft in the beam, grossed 470tons and had engines of only 120nhp. She must have seemed very insignificant and foolhardy as Johnston took her out of Falmouth with seventeen passengers on board on 16 August 1825. As it turned out the journey was to take 113 days of which about half were spent in steam. Although she did not fulfil the conditions attached to the offer of the prize, *Enterprise* was awarded half the prize money and was sold to the Government of Bengal. Another vessel, *Falcon* of 176tons and fitted with auxiliary steam power, is also recorded as sailing for Calcutta in 1825.

The East India Company is known to have been using steam by 1829 for on 20 March of that year *Hugh Lindsay*, a vessel of 410tons and 160nhp, sailed from Bombay where she had been built. Her destination was Aden, ten days steaming away. *Hugh Lindsay* had bunkers for only five and a half days supply and thus had to sail grossly overloaded and with every spare inch of space crammed with fuel. In fact it took this pioneer paddle steamer thirty-three days to cover nearly 3,000 miles but twelve days were spent coaling at Aden and Jedda. Despite the low average speed of the journey, the mail *Hugh Lindsay* carried reached England much quicker than it would have done via the Cape route and the vessel laid the foundation of a new line of communication to the east. The route improved even further in 1835 when the Admiralty packets established a reliable service between Malta and Alexandria and put the last link in the chain on a regular basis.

After her epic voyage from Falmouth *Enterprise* was used to carry dispatches between Calcutta and Burma during the First

Burmese War. From 1829 she worked in partnership with *Hugh Lindsay* until about 1836 when the pair were replaced by two more powerful consorts, *Atlanta* and *Berenice*.

One other vessel deserves mention among the ranks of the early ocean pioneers. This is the diminutive *Sophia Jane*. Once part of the fleet of the St George Steam Packet Company, *Sophia Jane* had the distinction of making the first steam voyage from Great Britain to Australia, in 1831.

CHAPTER FOUR

COAST AND ESTUARY

THE years between the advent of the paddle steamer and the dawn of the railway age were years of rapid and extensive change for Britain. Industry, under the impetus of steam and assisted by cheap canal transport, expanded quickly and over a wide area. In 1802, 168 furnaces produced 170,000tons of iron but by 1825 374 furnaces were at work and the production had risen to 581,367tons. With this sort of growth came more demand for improved transport for both business and pleasure purposes, a situation upon which the operators of steamer services were quick to capitalise.

Although the country was covered by a vast network of coach services these had little scope for further development in either speed or economy of operation. Fast passenger vessels on the canals helped to meet the demand and as steam vessels improved in comfort and reliability they began to draw traffic from a number of the coaching routes. Unlike the coaches, steamers did not pay any taxes and this factor, together with their relatively high capacity and the ability to sell wines and spirits without an excise licence, enabled the operators to charge attractive fares.

On routes affected by esturial and coastal steamer services both coach operators and the turnpike trusts began to lose money. Typical of the shorter routes affected was that from London to Maidstone. Here a coach fare of six shillings was charged, but by using the steamer service to Gravesend at a cost of only 1s 6d ($7\frac{1}{2}$p), a total of 2s (10p) could be saved on the journey. Not only did situations of this kind affect the coach operators' pockets and compel them to adjust their routes to cater for the steamer traffic, but also heightened their seasonal problem. Water travel declined sharply in popularity during the winter months compelling the coach firms to increase their own facilities and bring back into use vehicles which had lain idle during the summer.

The coaches also suffered at the hands of the coastal steamers which competed successfully for traffic between seaports and their hinterlands. A typical example of fare and journey comparisons in this sphere is afforded by the London to Newcastle route. Here coach operators charged inside passengers £4 10s (£4·50) and outside passengers exactly half this figure. By paddle steamer the journey could be accomplished for as little as forty shillings if one travelled in the fore cabin. This figure included sustenance en route and although the fare was not elaborate, obtaining meals on a coach journey could be quite an expensive business. The steamers charged only sixty shillings for the best cabins.

By coastal steamer a passenger could make the journey from London to Hull for 21s (£1·05) for a best cabin, 15s (75p) fore cabin. With the inside and outside coach fares to York 65s (£3·25) and 34s (£1·70) respectively even this route was not safe from the competition of the Hull steamers. The cost of coach travel was so high that it was bound to be vulnerable to competition. The 57-hour journey from London to Glasgow, for example, cost £10 8s (£10·40) for each passenger, £6 5s (£6·25) for each servant travelling outside, while £2 17s (£2·85) was needed for tips and then there was the cost of food and of luggage in excess of the 20lb free allowance.

In these conditions the development of steamer services in the estuaries was followed quickly by the introduction of paddle steamers on both traditional and new coastal routes. Leith was linked with London as early as 1821, with two 400ton vessels —each with sleeping accommodation for 100 passengers—operating the route and completing the journey in fifty hours. To reach Aberdeen added only another fourteen hours to the journey thus bringing the far north of the country within three days travelling of London. In 1822 the Plymouth, Devonport & Falmouth Steam Packet Company was formed to link the places named in its title and commenced doing so in 1823.

General Steam Navigation did a great deal of coasting trade using vessels like the wooden *Vivid* built by Curling & Young of Limehouse in 1835. For the first five years of her life the 428ton *Vivid*, which was engined by Seaward & Capel, worked between London and Hull for the Humber Union Steamship Company. Two years after passing into the hands of the GSN company this steamer collided with the steamer *Era* while carrying passengers to Greenwich. To save her passengers *Vivid* was run aground on the mud, but the unfortunate *Era* foundered at her moorings. Other GSN vessels on coastal work included the 206ft *Monarch* and the 766ton *Clarence* on the Edinburgh run, *Ramona* on the Yarmouth run and *London Merchant* which operated to Leith. In 1836 GSN took over the London & Edinburgh Steam Packet Company and its six steamers.

GSN's *London Merchant* was chartered by the Dundee, Perth & London Shipping Company when competition forced this concern into the steamer business. Previously the company had used only hired tugs and the steamer *Sir William Wallace* on local journeys between Dundee and Perth. The latter, introduced in 1829, not only towed lighters but also carried passengers at two shillings (10p) a time. In 1832 the company paid the Napier-Wood partnership £36,000 for two 300hp vessels, *Dundee* and *Perth*. Barquetine-rigged and with a black and red funnel, these steamers were 175ft long and had a beam measurement of 28ft. They were so successful that a third, slightly smaller vessel *London* was introduced in 1837 at a cost of £22,000.

Farther north the Aberdeen, Leith & Clyde Shipping Company introduced PS *Velocity* between Aberdeen and Leith in 1821 while in later years paddlers worked on services to Kirkwall and Lerwick. The Aberdeen Steam Navigation Company operated the 622ton *City of Aberdeen* which was built at Greenock in 1835 and was wrecked in 1871.

On the Humber were such vessels as the 152ft *Gazelle* and the ill-fated *Victoria* which suffered two successive boiler explosions in 1838. The former, which had been built at Greenock in 1832, belonged to the Hull & London Steam Packet Company while the latter, from the yard of J. North of Hull, was operated by the Hull Steam Shipping Company. The first explosion aboard *Victoria* occurred in March 1838 when the starboard boiler of the 240nhp Napier engines burst, killing three people and injuring several others. Only three months later the 698ton *Victoria* was in trouble again when she collided with a brig. The collision smashed the starboard paddle wheel and the vessel's strong head of steam, deprived of a legitimate means of escape, caused another explosion in which five people died.

Although the first paddle steamer in Northern Ireland appeared on Belfast Lough, a service on Lough Neagh followed soon after. The vessel concerned was the Lagan Navigation Company's *Marchioness of Donegal* built by Ritchie & MacLaine of Belfast and launched in 1821. Later vessels included *Grand Junction* built by Coates & Young of Belfast in 1842 and used between Portadown and Ballyronan. In the same year the *Countess of Erne* started work towing canal boats on Lough Erne and in 1843 *Lady of the Lake* commenced to ply between Sligo and Dromahaire on Lough Gill.

The rise of the paddle steamer was even more impressive on the Thames and the Clyde. On the former the period of greatest development was in the twenty years before the coming of the railways. Not that difficulties were not encountered. Where a wharf was used the wharfage dues were quite heavy at threepence per passenger and where no proper landing place existed there was constant strife between the watermen seeking fares at the various stairs which served the steamboats. The latter problem eased as new wharves were built in the thirties but the risk of accidents remained a problem for some time. Between the middle of 1835 and the end of 1838 twelve steamboats were seriously damaged in collisions, while forty-three people were drowned and five injured as a result of steamers upsetting other craft by reckless navigation.

In this pre-railway period the steamers carried virtually all the business between London, Gravesend, and Woolwich. The journey to Gravesend cost between one and sixpence (7½p) and two shillings (10p) and that to Woolwich half this price. The journey took up to ninety minutes against the tide and services continued throughout the winter and even after dark. At holiday times the traffic was exceptionally heavy and overcrowding became so dangerous that in September 1835 the Lord Mayor's Court approved by-laws limiting vessels to three passengers per registered ton. Even so, the Woolwich Steam Packet Company still carried a quarter of a million passengers in a typical year's operation. This company had been established in 1834 and maintained a regular day service between Charing Cross Wharf and Strothers Wharf at Woolwich, calling at Greenwich and Greenhithe en route. It operated such vessels as *Nymph*, *Fairy*, and *Naiad*.

Other companies operating downstream from London Bridge included the rival Diamond and Star companies. There was intense competition between pairs of vessels belonging to these two, with the Star company's *Comet* vying with the Diamond steamer *Ruby*. The latter, which was built by Wallis of Blackwall two years after *Comet* was launched at Rotherhithe in 1834, dealt a severe blow to the Star company. Of 243tons gross and fitted with Seaward engines of 110nhp, *Ruby* was capable of a speed of thirteen knots which made her popular with passengers and difficult to beat.

Up-river services had been among the earliest but had not developed at the same rate as those below London Bridge. A Gravesend to Richmond service was operated by ps *Kent* which came from Baukham's yard at Gravesend, but the real expansion started in 1837. From that date small steamers capable of carrying 120 passengers started operating a fifteen-minute service from 8am to 9pm between London, Southwark, and Westminster bridges at a fare of fourpence. In the following year the Iron Steam Boat Company introduced a further similar service but running from London Bridge to Waterloo and Westminster bridges and to the new railway terminus at Nine Elms. In 1846 the Citizen Steamboat Company joined in and the Dyers Hall Company started a halfpenny service from its wharf near London

Bridge to the Adelphi using small steamers bearing such names as *Ant, Cricket,* and *Fly.*

Once the railway age dawned, steamers lost much of the business they had taken from the coaches. On the Thames, the first railway to challenge the steamers was an enterprise entitled the London & Blackwall Railway & Steam Navigation Depot which promoted a line from the city with the express object of capturing the horse bus and steamer traffic to a rail/steamer route via its Brunswick Wharf at Blackwall.

The new railway was opened from the Minories to Blackwall on 6 July 1840 and was later extended to a terminus at Fenchurch Street. Three vessels, *Railway, Brunswick,* and *Blackwall,* were obtained from the local firm of Ditchburn & Mare and the two brought into operation in 1841 had carried 140,500 passengers by the end of that year. *Brunswick,* as a typical example of the three, was 158ft long and of 258 gross tons. Her 90ihp engines were of Seaward's direct-acting type, while *Railway* had two-cylinder oscillating engines of the same rating by J. Penn & Sons and *Blackwall* a single-cylinder steeple engine supplied by Miller & Ravenhill. As railways had no powers to operate steamships at this period the three vessels were worked in conjunction with the Star company.

At first the new railway had its share of troubles with its cable haulage system constantly breaking down and the steamer companies showing a reluctance to surrender their through traffic. However, matters began to improve slowly. First the Woolwich company agreed to provide a fifteen-minute service from Brunswick Wharf to Woolwich and then *Father Thames* and *Sons of the Thames* of the Sons of the Thames Company were reported as coming into the railway fold.

A notorious paddler using Brunswick Wharf was the 180ft *Prince of Wales,* an iron vessel built at Deptford in 1841. This steamer had a Miller & Ravenhill inverted beam engine taken from one of the old Ramsgate boats. Although her maximum speed is recorded as fourteen knots *Prince of Wales* had a reputation as a very fast vessel largely due to the reckless and inconsiderate way in which she was handled. Complaints about her wash were frequent and on one occasion she swamped a small trading schooner. In 1862 *Prince of Wales* collided with the yacht *Marina*. Another vessel which came to use Brunswick Wharf was the 160ft Greenwich-built steamer *Queen* which was reputed to have a speed of seventeen knots.

About this time there was great excitement on the river when the *Red Rover*, which had been built in 1838 for the Herne Bay Steam Packet Company, was modernised and then tested against the screw steamer *Mermaid*. The latter had just been fitted with a propeller of Rennie's patent and the test aroused much attention. It turned out to be exciting but inconclusive. Over the ten-mile course from Long Reach Tavern to Gravesend *Mermaid* proved the winner by some three hundred yards.

A Blackwall Railway report mentions that in 1841 the journey time between Blackwall and Gravesend was as little as seventy minutes with the tide and thirty-five minutes longer against it. Operating from Brunswick Wharf the steamers were able to accomplish six journeys per day and so charge fares which were only a third of the through fare from London Bridge. At the height of the competitive period express trains operated from Fenchurch Street to Blackwall and no sooner were the passengers on board the steamer than she would be off at full speed and the fires not eased until the vessel lay alongside Gravesend pier.

At first the Diamond company's boats did not call at Blackwall and the route was left to the rival Star company's *Jupiter*, *Mars*, and *Venus*. Competition was originally fierce too between the Woolwich and Waterman companies. The latter company comprised a group of Thames watermen who found that the only way to beat the steamer movement was to join it. No less than thirteen vessels bore the name *Waterman* and although the original rivalries were bitter, by 1847 the two companies had settled down to operating an alternate fifteen-minute service from Blackwall to Woolwich. The Waterman company eventually absorbed its rival.

There were, of course, other companies and vessels operating on the Thames at this period although the local traffic began to diminish as the railways expanded. The Greenwich Steam Packet Company operated a service from London Bridge Wharf to Greenwich with the PS *Greenwich*. Built at Poplar in 1835 this vessel one year later collided with the *Royal Tar* of Dublin and nearly sank, her passengers being taken off by the *Fly*.

The development on the Clyde was quite as rapid as that on the Thames and 168 steamers had been built by 1850. Prior to this the rivalry between the operators had grown to an intense pitch and several incidents resulted. These included explosions on *Telegraph* and *Plover* and the wrecking of *Countess of Eglinton* at Millport in 1846. The first rail and steamer link via Greenock and the Glasgow, Paisley & Greenock Railway was introduced in 1844 and although it eventually failed due to the cheap through steamer fares and the necessity for changing, it had revealed the shape of things to come.

Not only did the number of steamers and number of services on the Clyde expand, but so did the facilities for this waterborne traffic. This process started as early as 1822 when a £600 harbour facility was brought into use at Rothesay. Prior to this the town had only had the eleventh century quay and passengers were normally landed by rowing boat. For a long time passengers for private houses adjacent to the steamer route could be met and landed by their own rowing boat, but gradually proper landing facilities were provided at the main ports of call. David Napier had a hand in improving the facilities. He not only applied his talents to engineering, but also built a pier at Kilmun in 1828 and generally contributed to the development of the area, putting the steamer *Marion* on Loch Lomond and the *Aglaia* on Loch Eck. Other improvements of this period included a subscription pier at Millport in 1833 and a £4,275 quay at Largs in the following year. Another round of improvements came in the eleven years from Strone pier in 1847 to Hunters Quay in 1858.

The 1830s and 40s were a busy and colourful period in the

Page 51: *(above)* Built by Curling & Young at Limehouse in 1838, *British Queen* was the largest vessel afloat at the time of her launch; *(below)* the PS *Enterprise* of 1824 was the first paddle steamer to reach India

Page 52: (above) Three paddle steamers of the Woolwich Steam Packet Company with PS *Nymph* in the foreground; (below) the 300ton PS *Monarch* of the Isle of Man & Liverpool Steam Navigation Company

paddle steamer's history. The wharves and landing places were crowded and exciting. Fleets tended to be small until the growth of the railways forced amalgamations, and each owner, wharf superintendent, or agent spared no effort to draw attention to the superior nature of his own facilities. St Katherine's Wharf in London vaunted its approaches of 'unexampled Convenience' for passengers for the 'elegantly-fitted and commodious steam packets' sailing with 'undeviating punctuality' to places such as Margate, Ipswich, Redcar, and Leith. Some steamers relied on speed, others on catering, comfort, or entertainment. In 1833 the *Albion* offered 'a concert, a wonderful illusionist, a ball and an efficient band', while the *Vesta* of 1841 relied on its fine meals, including a handsome dinner for 1s 6d ($7\frac{1}{2}$p).

With the further expansion of the railway network, some change in the pattern of paddle steamer services was inevitable. Increasing emphasis came to be placed on the excursion and pleasure rôle of the steamers and by 1840 in the south, not only had Southend pier been in use for six years but GSN had started calling at Herne Bay and the Medway Steam Packet Company had come into being. Examples of rail-steamer co-operation showed that the steamers were l arning to live with and even benefit from the railways. As an illustration, after the railway opened to Gravesend, for 2s 6d ($12\frac{1}{2}$p) Londoners could travel by steamer to that point, visit the famous Rosherville Gardens and return by rail.

Even where there was no scope or no inclination for co-operation the steamer operators did not give in tamely. When Yarmouth and Norwich got their rail link with London in 1845 the Norfolk Steam Packet Company was advertising reduced fares on its weekly service from Yarmouth to London and the two paddlers on the Yarmouth–Norwich service were offering a fare of ninepence for the trip to Yarmouth races. When the Great Northern Railway opened its route from Boston to Lincoln, the packet steamer company cut its fare by half, but in 1850 the GNR retaliated with a fare of only 1s 3d (6p) and the river traffic slowly died until it ceased altogether in 1863. The coal traffic

D

transferred from sea-going vessels to the inland rivers and drains via the Grand Sluice at Boston dropped from 19,535 tons in 1847 to 3,780 tons in 1853.

But as the paddler gave some ground on local services, it grew in importance on the short sea routes.

CHAPTER FIVE

SHORT SEA SERVICES

THE rapid expansion of steamer services on the Clyde led directly to the introduction of steamers on the short sea routes, especially those of the nearby Irish Sea. In the same year that Napier put *Rob Roy* onto a Greenock to Belfast service, the paddle steamer *Hibernia* started to work between Howth and Holyhead. Also, in 1816 the paddle steamers *Waterloo* and *Belfast* began alternate day sailings between Liverpool and Dublin. Three years later Messrs Langtry of Belfast acquired the former for £10,000 and put her to work between Liverpool and Belfast. Then *Belfast* took over the working in July 1820.

The year 1819 was also a momentous one. On 2 August the first steamship appeared on the Liverpool–Glasgow route. This was the paddler *Robert Burns* which operated the service from Greenock calling at Portpatrick and Douglas en route to Liverpool and taking thirty hours on the journey. This time, achieved on a regular basis, was quite startling by sailing packet standards. It brought something of a crisis to the mail arrangements of the Post Office which was still using the traditional sailing packets.

Matters came to a head when the New Steam Packet Company put two paddle steamers on the Holyhead to Dublin route. These two vessels, the 170ton *Ivanhoe* and the slightly smaller *Talbot*, completed the journey in about eight and a half hours, half the time taken by the Post Office sailing vessels. The attitude of the Post Office to mail contracts was constantly changing in response to internal and external influences but at this period the policy was to compete. Accordingly the Post Office had two vessels built on the Thames specifically for the Holyhead mail route. *Lightning* was of 205tons and 80hp, while the second of the two challengers, *Meteor,* was a slightly smaller vessel of 189tons and 60hp. The two steamers were completed in May 1821 and steamed round to their new homes with their Holyhead crews keyed up for the competition which lay ahead.

Talbot and *Ivanhoe* had queened the Holyhead to Dublin route for two years, but the newcomers had the advantage of size and of two years of improvements in design and machinery. On her first trip in June 1821, *Meteor* showed a clean pair of heels to *Talbot.* Next, *Lightning* cheekily sailed out to meet the incoming *Ivanhoe* and promptly raced her into port. With faster vessels now operating on the service all the passenger traffic which had flooded to the New Steam Packet Company when the service was inaugurated transferred back to the mail ships. The New Steam Packet Company vessels were withdrawn and, by a piece of final irony, *Ivanhoe* later returned to the route after being purchased by the Post Office as a third vessel.

From this time onwards expansion was rapid. In 1821 the Cambrian Steam Packet Company increased its sailings between Liverpool and Bagillt on the Dee estuary with the steamer *Cambria* and the *Britannia* started working from the Clyde to the Giant's Causeway. Later this vessel operated a weekly run between Glasgow and Londonderry. Also in 1821 two of the largest and most powerful vessels on the Irish Sea were put into operation between Liverpool and Douglas. These were the steamers *St Patrick* and *St George.*

In 1822 the 240ton *Eclipse* and the *Superb* with its two 35hp engines joined *Robert Burns* on the Liverpool–Greenock run. The latter, a 150ton vessel, had two engines of 30hp. In the same year a Liverpool to Cork service was inaugurated by the St George Steam Packet Company.

The whole period was one of constant development with the new method of sea travel dramatically changing the previous situation. Some of the old companies like Langtrys turned successfully to steam, while others went to the wall. New companies sprang up, some sound, some mainly speculative. In 1824 the City of Dublin Steam Packet Company joined the St George and St Patrick companies in providing services to Southern Ireland by introducing the 130hp paddler *City of Dublin* from the yards of the famous 'Frigate' Wilson. By 1826, despite its rivals, the new company was operating more than a dozen steamers and was also serving Drogheda, Belfast, and Londonderry. It was in that year that the company introduced the *Thames* and *Shannon*, both of 180ft, 513tons burden and with engines of 160hp. After working from Ireland to Liverpool *Shannon* went on a Dublin to London service and lasted until 1848 despite a bad fire on board two years earlier. A similar vessel, *City of Londonderry*, was also added to the fleet about 1826, the three vessels normally taking eighty hours on their journey to London.

The new services from Liverpool to Dublin allowed the Liverpool merchants to dispatch their mail much later than was possible via the Holyhead route. This was because the latter meant using a connecting coach to link up with the London mail at Chester. The improved service did much to further Liverpool's claim to packet port status. Another step was taken with the introduction of regular sailings to the Isle of Man. The steamer services, which operated twice weekly in summer and once weekly in winter, provided a much quicker total journey time than the mail route using the Whitehaven sailing packets. By this time private competition had forced the Post Office to convert further routes to steamer operation including those from Weymouth and Milford Haven.

The Irish Sea had become steadily more competitive with rival companies slashing rates and trying to outspeed their competitors in a bid to win the available traffic. Competition was particularly fierce on the Glasgow to Belfast route and by 1825 had gone so far that the first-class fare was down to two shillings (10p) and deck passengers were being carried free.

A well-known paddle steamer operating between Glasgow and Belfast was the *Frugal* built in 1826. *Frugal* was 116ft long and had a beam of 21·5ft and a draught of 12·33ft. Powered by two engines of 50hp, this vessel sailed from Glasgow each Tuesday and Friday. She had thirty passenger berths and accommodation for 180 tons of cargo as well as carrying horse boxes on deck. Twenty shillings was charged for a cabin, deck passengers paying three shillings (15p).

To meet the competition from the Glasgow–Belfast steamers the Post Office transferred *Arrow* and *Dasher* from the Dover station to Portpatrick. These vessels, which had started sailing to and from Calais as early as 1821, were replaced at Dover by *Spitfire* and *Fury*. Although the Post Office granted a private contract for the conveyance of the Isle of Man mails it adhered, in the main, to a policy of owning mail vessels. This was to be criticised in a report of 1830 largely on the grounds that the receipts were only half the expenses. Nevertheless the situation remained unchanged until 1836 when a report of the Commissioners of Revenue recommended that Admiralty brigs should take over the work as they had done at Falmouth back in 1823.

Another route which went through a period of keen competition about this time was that between Belfast and Liverpool. Langtrys had hardly got nicely established on this route with their steamers carrying the passengers and the older smacks the cargo when competition appeared in the form of the Belfast Steam Packet Company which was formed by a number of Belfast merchants in 1824. This company's 194ton *Shamrock*, which made her maiden voyage on 5 December 1824, was taken over in 1826 by the City of Dublin Steam Packet Company. *Shamrock*, with *Sheffield* and the 210ton *Hibernia*, was soon challenged by Langtry's 411ton *Chieftain* which had been built by Ritchie and provided with 150hp engines by Victor Coates.

By this time the network of steamer services crossing the Irish sea was extensive, the vessels catering not only for the traditional business provided by the travel needs of government and commerce, but stimulating new traffics by their reliable services and economic rates. The export of Irish cattle, as an example, derived a tremendous boost from the advent of the paddle steamer.

With business growing and the steamboat fleets expanding, too much was at stake for competition to remain within sensible limits. In the case of Langtrys and the Dublin company fares were brought as low as threepence, including the provision of bread and meat, before the competing parties accepted that this course could only ruin them both. The outcome was a traffic-sharing agreement which gave Langtrys two-thirds of the traffic and the Dublin company the remainder.

Prior to the advent of steamers the main route to and from the Isle of Man was via Whitehaven and a weekly cutter which took six hours on the journey. When *Robert Bruce* started her regular summer-only sailings in 1819 the journey to Liverpool took ten hours, but the following year brought improvements both in the service and in speed when James Little of Greenock put *Majestic* and *City of Glasgow* on the Greenock–Liverpool run. By this time steamers sailed from each end of the route on Mondays, Wednesdays, and Fridays and the journey time between Liverpool and the Isle of Man was reduced to nine hours. By 1822 not only were *Eclipse* and *Superb* also calling at Douglas but in the May of that year the St George Steam Packet Company of Liverpool was using its fine paddle steamer *St George* and competing successfully with the Little vessels.

After a period *St George* was transferred to the Irish station and was replaced by the *Sophia Jane*, one of several Irish Sea vessels which was destined for greater things. By this time quite a few vessels were calling at the island on their journey between Liverpool and the Clyde, including at least five steamers belonging to Liverpool companies and several more owned in Scotland. In addition the steamer *St Andrew* worked between Whitehaven, Douglas, and Dublin and the *George IV* operated from Liverpool to Douglas and Warrenport.

In 1825 the steamer *Triton*, a tiny vessel of 30tons, took over the carriage of the mails from the Whitehaven cutters but sailing vessels continued to carry the bigger part of the island's goods and passenger traffic for another eight or nine years. Three years later the mail contract passed to the St George company but although the Manx service was satisfactory in summer with plenty of vessels operating and the fares very low in consequence, matters were very different in the winter. Then only the St George company remained on the route and it used only its smallest and oldest vessels, steamers like *Prince Llewellyn*, originally intended for a service from Liverpool to Beaumaris, Bangor, and Caernarvon, *St David* of 180tons and 75hp, and *Lady Abbess*.

The Manx people were not satisfied with these conditions and tried to establish their own steamer service. The idea was first tried in 1826 when consideration was given to buying the steamer *Victory*. This scheme fell through and the 112ton *Victory*, together with her sister ship *Harriet*, continued to work for her Liverpool owners until the former was acquired by Captain, later Sir, John Ross for his expedition in search of the North West Passage. The idea had more success in 1829 and the Isle of Man Steam Packet Company was born at a meeting held in the December of that year when £4,500 was subscribed towards the purchase of a steamboat. The new company was called the Mona's Isle Company and its first vessel was the 200ton *Mona's Isle* obtained from John Wood of Glasgow for £7,052. Engined by Robert Napier, whose reputation she further enhanced, *Mona's Isle* came near to beating *Sophia Jane* on her first run from Douglas to Liverpool and later outstripped her opponent regularly.

This new competition brought on a fares war with the St George company bringing its fares down as low as sixpence. All this achieved was an increase in the number of undesirable characters using the service and the next move was to bring *St George* back from her Irish station to meet the new challenge. *St George* lost the first race because Captain Gill of *Mona's Isle* was smart enough to distribute his cargo so as to keep both paddles biting when the wind would otherwise have lifted one out of the water. Shortly afterwards *St George* foundered in a gale in Douglas Bay when her cable parted as she lay at anchor.

The smaller and slower steamers of the St George company were soon forced off the route and while competition from a steamer called *William the Fourth* continued for a short while, the Manx company had no real opposition. In 1832 came the company's second steamer *Mona* which was smaller but slightly faster than her companion from the Wood shipyards. As a contemporary writer put it 'her motions are, if possible, superior in celerity'. *Mona* operated both to Liverpool and to Whitehaven taking seven and a half hours for the former journey and four hours, thirty-five minutes for the latter. The year of her acquisition also saw the company change its name, first to the Isle of Man United Steam Packet Company and then to the present title.

The diminutive 98ft *Mona* was followed by the 128ft *Queen of the Isle* obtained from Robert Napier in 1834. Shortly after this a splinter group of the main company broke away and formed the Isle of Man & Liverpool Steam Navigation Company which started operating in 1836, first the *Clyde* and then a new 300ton vessel built by Steele of Greenock and named *Monarch*. *Queen of the Isle* had already shown a clean pair of heels to all the Liverpool steamers including the very fast Government packet *Richmond*, but she met a worthy opponent in *Monarch* and the racing honours were fairly evenly shared. The competition meant low fares of two shillings and sixpence (12½p) cabin and one shilling (5p) steerage and in 1837 the owners of *Monarch* went out of business leaving the original company in undisturbed possession of the route.

The little *Mona* was sold in 1841 to end up as a tug in Dublin Bay and in the following year the company acquired the 433ton *King Orry* from John Winram's yard at Douglas. This vessel brought the Douglas to Liverpool time down to below seven hours before being disposed of to Napier in part payment for *Douglas* (I). She ultimately went to the eastern Mediterranean. Two other vessels joined the fleet before the century passed the halfway point. The first was *Ben-my-Chree* which took *Queen of the Isle*'s engines when the latter was converted to a full-rigged sailing ship. She was followed in 1846 by *Tynwald* (I) which, at 700tons, was nearly twice the size of her predecessors.

Although the St George company relinquished the Isle of Man traffic to its Manx rivals, the company continued to grow. By

1834 it was operating from Liverpool to Cork, to Plymouth and to London, to Dublin, Dundalk, and Newry, from London to Exeter and Cork via Cowes, from Bristol to Cork and Dublin, from Glasgow and Greenock to Dublin and Newry, and from Dublin to Cork, Waterford, and Newry.

The growth of traffic and companies on the Irish Sea was also apparent elsewhere. On the Humber, the history of steamer operation which stretched back to 1814 and an 1816 service between Hull and Gainsborough blossomed in October 1817 into a London to Hull service and by 1826 some twenty-four steamers were sailing from the port. Nine years later this number had increased to forty with sailings as far afield as Holland.

In the English Channel the early pioneers were soon followed by regular services. Initially these crossings took about three and a half hours and although this was no faster than the sailing vessels, the steamers were considerably more reliable. The carriage of mails on this route followed the usual pattern. At first the mails were in the hands of privately-owned steamers like *Sprite* but they were later transferred to the Post Office steamers. This arrangement lasted until the Admiralty took over the work in 1837. By this time the cross-channel journey had been reduced to three hours, the privately-owned *Firefly* first achieving this time in 1830.

On the east coast, short sea services from London became almost synonymous with the name of the General Steam Navigation Company. One of the earliest companies to operate paddle steamers, the GSN came into being in 1824 when Mr William John Hall combined his London to Hull vessels with the steamer *Eagle* which Mr Thomas Brocklebank had been operating between London and Margate. A joint stock company was formed embracing others with interests in the Margate trade and with a prospectus which declared :

> The National benefits resulting from the power of steam are so universally acknowledged, that it appears unnecessary to dwell upon its many advantages. By its application, ships are enabled to enter and quit Harbours regardless of winds or tides, and it

affords the most flattering prospects of connecting the remotest parts of the Globe by a more safe and rapid communication

The first act of the new company was to purchase two steam packets, the *Lord Melville* and the *Earl of Liverpool*. Orders were also placed for three steamers, each of 240tons and with two engines of 40hp, for working from Brighton to Dieppe and on the London to Yarmouth and London to Rotterdam runs. The year 1825 saw the inception of a service from Brighton to Havre and Dieppe and of a connection between Havre and Portsmouth. Services from London to Dunkirk, Hamburg, Ostend, and Calais were introduced and the traffic in cattle to Holland was expanded. These were years of considerable expansion with fifteen steamers working in 1824, a further five in 1825, and eight more in 1826.

A handbill of 1826 shows that the 124ft *Lord Melville* under the command of Captain Middleton and the 147ft *Attwood* under Captain Stranack were working between London and Calais four days each week, while the original 262ton *Earl of Liverpool* was doing the sixteen-hour voyage to Ostend along with *Mountaineer* on Wednesdays and Saturdays. Two steamers, *George IV* and *Duke of York* both of 760tons and 150hp, worked from London to Lisbon, Oporto, Vigo, and Gibraltar and were advertised as being prepared to pick up off Brighton and at Portsmouth those who could not start the journey from Deptford. *Rapid* was working the Deptford to Boulogne run twice a week, while the 204ton *Belfast* sailed to and from Rotterdam and the Hamburg service was in the hands of *Sir Edward Banks* and *Hylton Jolliffe*. *Eclipse, Talbot,* and *Quentin Durward* operated a Monday to Friday service between Brighton and Dieppe.

Fares shown on the 1826 bill ranged from thirty shillings (£1·50) for a fore cabin from Brighton to Dieppe to £31 10s (£31·50) for a chief cabin to Lisbon. The journey from London to Margate or Ramsgate cost twelve shillings (60p) for a chief cabin, ten shillings (50p) for a fore cabin and three guineas (£3·15) for what is described as a season ticket 'with the privilege of the Ramsgate and Margate packets'. Servants and children under twelve were charged six shillings (30p). Four vessels operated this route, with sailings to Margate at nine o'clock every morning except Sunday and to Ramsgate every Wednesday and Saturday at eight o'clock.

In 1828, a year in which eighty steamships were classed in Lloyds Register, GSN introduced first a Portsmouth to Bordeaux run and later a Southampton–Plymouth–Bordeaux service. In the following year came the honour of royal patronage when the Empress of Brazil travelled from Ostend to London in the company's 125ton paddle steamer *Superb*. In 1832 GSN arranged with Dover coach proprietors for daily coaches from Dover, Deal, and Sandwich to meet the packets at Margate.

There was another period of expansion from 1834 onwards with twenty-three vessels being introduced before 1840. GSN's Margate rivals and the London & Edinburgh Steam Packet Company were taken over during the same period bringing the company's fleet up to forty vessels including one stationed at Falmouth to receive letters from wind-bound boats. By this time there were short sea services to and from London, Antwerp, Havre, Boulogne, Dieppe, Calais, Hamburg, Ostend, and Rotterdam and coastal services to Berwick, Leith, Newcastle, Sunderland, Ipswich, Margate, Ramsgate, and Herne Bay.

GSN continued to expand in the 1840s with sixteen new vessels being acquired. The company's first iron paddler was the 407ton *Rainbow* of 1838 and the last wooden paddler the 395ton *Perth* of 1861. In between, wood and iron construction alternated with vessels ranging in size from the 175ton *Magician* of 1844 to the 872ton *Monarch* of 1850.

CHAPTER SIX

TRANSATLANTIC HEYDAY

THE year 1838 was a significant one in the history of steam voyages across the Atlantic. The rapid spread of the steamer on the shorter routes and the historic voyages of *Sirius* and *Great Western* had helped to convince the Admiralty of the merits of steam vessels for the conveyance of mails. The result was that in November 1838 tenders were invited for the steamer carriage of the mail traffic between Britain and North America.

In a way the story of this period really starts back on the day in 1831 when the first *Royal William* was launched from a ship-yard at Three Rivers, Quebec to have her British engines installed at St Mary's Foundry, Montreal. This 176ft pioneer sailed from Pictou, Nova Scotia on 18 August 1833 and although she had only seven passengers on board she more than made up for this by having 144 backers including Samuel Cunard. A gale off Newfoundland disabled *Royal William*'s starboard engine, but she reached Gravesend on 12 September after undergoing repairs at Cowes. Apart from the one day out of four devoted to clearing her boilers of salt scale, this diminutive paddler had steamed continuously and her voyage made a great impression on Cunard.

When the Admiralty advertisement appeared, Cunard's long-standing interest in steamships quickened. The contract conditions involved a monthly mail service between either Liverpool, Bristol, Plymouth, Falmouth, or Southampton and Halifax and between Halifax and New York. Steam vessels of not less than 300hp were stipulated and two tenders were submitted. The St George Steam Packet Company, owners of the *Sirius*, offered a service from Cork with smaller vessels to be used between there and Liverpool and on the New York leg. The Great Western Steamship Company proposed a monthly service between Bristol and Halifax with 1,000ton iron vessels or 1,500ton wooden vessels. Neither company was ready to commence operating immediately and thus their tenders did not fulfil the conditions of the contract.

Meanwhile Cunard had sailed to England and through the secretary of the East India Company, for which he was an agent, had contacted Robert Napier, George Burns the Glasgow shipowner, and David MacIver of Liverpool. With the advice and co-operation of these three leading personalities in the steam shipping world, Cunard was able to present acceptable proposals to the Admiralty. Then, with Burns and MacIver as partners, he formed the British & North American Royal Mail Steam Packet Company. Robert Napier's technical contribution was recognised by contracts to provide engines for the Cunard vessels.

Much organising had to be done before regular sailings could start. Not only had the new company financial and commercial matters to arrange, but also many practical details associated with victualling and coal bunkering and with tender and harbour facilities. This was a new and important prestige service. It had a promise to live up to, a reputation to build and keen competition to contend with.

The forerunner of the new fleet was the ps *Unicorn* which had been built by Robert Steele & Son at Greenock in 1836 for G. & J. Burns' service between Glasgow and Liverpool. Of 648tons gross register and 185ft long, *Unicorn* was carvel-built as a three-masted schooner. She sailed from Liverpool on 16 May 1840 to make dockage arrangements at Boston before working the Pictou to Quebec branch of the route. Later in her life this handsome vessel worked between Panama and San Francisco and then crossed the Pacific to Australia.

Unicorn was followed by four larger vessels all built by Robert Duncan & Co at Greenock and all engined by Robert Napier. These were *Britannia*, *Acadia*, *Caledonia*, and *Columbia*. *Britannia* was slightly longer than the other three but otherwise the dimensions of the four vessels were very similar. She was also the first to be built and was launched on 5 February 1840.

In his *American Notes* Charles Dickens describes his voyage to Boston on *Britannia* and brings to life the nature and events of an early steam crossing. His description of the accommodation is notably less enthusiastic than the official reference to luxurious cabins for 115 passengers. Even so the 'garden-stuff, pale sucking pigs, calves heads in scores' which were brought aboard must have made the journey idyllic compared with the lot of those who were forced to cross in the main cabin of a sailing vessel and provide their own provisions. Stewards, surgeon, butcher, and baker were included in the eighty-nine officers and men to run the vessel and care for the passengers and although the ladies' rooms were swept at 5am, at least the bar was opened only one hour later!

A three-masted barque of 1,156tons, with a square stern and a clipper bow with a long, plain bowsprit, *Britannia* was 228ft long and had a beam of 34·3ft. She earned a Blue Riband with her first crossing on 4 July 1840 using her Napier 440nhp side-lever engines whose two cylinders were supplied with steam at 9psi from four return-flue boilers, each with three furnaces. The paddles were 28ft in diameter and had 21 fixed radial floats revolving at 16rpm to produce a normal speed of 8·5knots. The vessel had bunkers for 640tons of coal and her engines consumed 37tons per day. After completing forty Atlantic crossings *Britannia* was sold to Germany in 1849 for conversion to a warship.

At this period there were two Cunard crossings each month for eight months of the year, on the fourth and fourteenth of each month. During the winter months only the first of the two crossings operated. *Acadia* started work by making the second of the monthly crossings and both this vessel and her sister ship *Columbia* created new records in the process of setting up a regular and reliable service. The latter was wrecked off Cape Sable during a homeward voyage but all lives and all the mail was saved. The 1,139ton *Acadia* was sold to Germany along with

Britannia in 1849, while in the following year *Caledonia* was sold to Spanish owners for £35,000 and was then wrecked in 1851.

The first Cunard vessels were not altogether a financial success, but apart from this Cunard went from strength to strength, adding to his services several new branches and several new vessels. The new destinations included Bermuda, the West Indies, and Newfoundland and the new vessels, *Hibernia* and *Cambria* of over 1,400tons. *Hibernia* was 248ft long and had two-cylinder Napier side-lever engines of 500nhp. Launched in 1843, four years later she made a record crossing from Halifax to Liverpool to claim the Blue Riband with an average speed of 11·67knots. By 1850 *Hibernia* had become outmoded and she was sold to the Spanish Government for use as a naval vessel. *Cambria*, which had been launched in 1845 also from Steele's Greenock yard, lasted until 1854 when she saw Admiralty service as a troopship in the Crimean war.

Hibernia anticipated a fresh Admiralty contract for a service to New York by sailing on to that port from Boston at the end of 1847. This contract, providing for a route to New York and one to Halifax and Boston, went to Cunard despite the existence of a Select Committee considering mail services and some popular feeling against the apparent preference for an American-led company. Although the Great Western company had added the 3,200ton screw-driven *Great Britain* to its fleet it was again an unsuccessful tenderer and gave up the struggle, selling *Great Western* to the Royal Mail Line and *Great Britain* for use in the Australian trade.

Descriptions available of these times picture a crowded hectic scene on sailing day. The main deck was the centre of activity with the passengers, livestock, coal, and stores being sorted into their proper places. The passenger cabins were on the lower deck but the officers' cabins were usually grouped aft with another set of cabins for the purser and similar functionaries lining the paddle boxes. If the main saloon was on the main deck, the poop deck above housed the steering position with an officer at the binnacle to instruct the helmsman. This officer received his instructions from the main control position either on the paddle box or near to it. Here too would be a wire leading to a bell in the engine room and used for conveying signals to the engineers, the captain using this and his speaking trumpet as his main means of control. Milk on board came from a cow, while fresh vegetables and other provisions were kept in the ice houses on the better vessels. On others they were kept in any odd corner and even, on occasions, under the lifeboats. Coaling was the biggest problem of all with large tonnages having to be loaded by barrow or skip.

Fares had started at thirty-five guineas (£36·75) to Halifax and thirty-nine (£40·95) to Boston with wines and spirits provided in addition to food. Eastbound, the prevailing winds reduced the advantage of the steamer over the sailing packets and a common fare of 125 dollars (£25) applied. As the popularity of the steamer services increased, the sailing frequencies doubled and fares rose to forty-one guineas (£43·05) before the advent of American competition set them tumbling.

America was not content to leave the British in general or Cunard in particular with the steamer monopoly of the Atlantic or to continue to rely on her lead in sailing ships although many still preferred this means of travel. In 1847 *Washington* and *Hermann* of the Ocean Steam Navigation Company started to follow in the path of the *Savannah*. These vessels operated on the New York, Southampton, and Bremen route and their owners became known as the Bremen Line. In the following year the PS *Franklin* pioneered a service to France with a call at the Isle of Wight. The *Franklin*'s owners, the New York & Havre Steam Navigation Company, were called the Havre Line.

In 1848 Cunard added four more vessels to the fleet, *America*, *Canada*, and *Niagara* built by Steele & Sons, and *Europa* from the yard of John Wood & Co. They were three-masted barques and *America*, at 251ft long and of 1,825tons, was typical of her sisters. Her engines, of 670nhp and 1,400ihp, gave an indication in their size of how times had changed. They continued to be of

E

the side-lever type but the two cylinders were 88·5in diameter by 96in stroke. Steam was supplied at 18psi from iron flue boilers with 4,750sq ft of heating surface and 16 furnaces of 300sq ft grate area. Sixty tons of coal was consumed daily in producing *America*'s normal speed of ten knots.

Europa, which was disposed of in 1867, made some very fast crossings in her early years. Less savoury claims to fame were the mishap in which she ran down the brig *Charles Bartlett* in fog and the later collision with *Arabia*. *Canada*, which had raised the average crossing speed to 12·23knots in 1849, was disposed of in the same year as *Europa*. Like *America* which was sold in 1863, she became a sailing vessel. *Niagara*, sold in 1866, became a sailer in the Australian trade and was wrecked in June 1875.

Edward K. Collins of the Dramatic Line of sailing vessels had persuaded Congress in November 1847 to grant a subsidy of 385,000 dollars annually towards a New York–Liverpool service promised to be at least as fast as that of the Cunard vessels. His United States Mail Steamship Company then had four vessels built for the service, each of some 2,856tons and with engines of 2,000hp. The 300ft *Atlantic* was the first of the four and was launched in April 1849. She cost 675,000 dollers and this high figure resulted in Congress raising the subsidy in 1852 to 858,000 dollars, this to cover twenty-six round voyages each year.

On 27 May 1850 *Atlantic* left New York on her maiden voyage which she completed on 10 June. *Pacific* entered the service in the September and in the following year achieved a record passage of nine days and just over twenty hours between New York and Liverpool. This meant the loss of one Blue Riband by Cunard, the other falling to the Collins Line in the same year.

The first response to the Collins challenge by the British & North American Company was two more wooden vessels from Steele's yards in 1850 and a third in 1852. These were *Asia* and *Africa* of 2,226tons and then *Arabia*. *Asia* was noted as a fast vessel and on the return section of her maiden voyage she took only nine days and fourteen hours for the crossing from Boston.

Later she made a record east to west crossing to Halifax of eight days, seventeen hours. Her coal consumption was 76tons per day, while her bunkering capacity of 930tons compared with a cargo capacity of only 500tons.

The 266ft *Africa* holed herself on a rock in October 1851 but was not seriously damaged. Her engines, reboilered in 1857, were of the usual Napier side-lever, jet-condensing type. They were rated at 3000ihp compared with the 740ihp rating of *Acadia* which had been built ten years earlier. Although on one crossing *Asia* produced an average speed of 12·36knots, all three vessels were laid down before the full measure of the Collins competition was realised and they proved no match for the American vessels in speed. *Arabia* was sold out of Cunard service in 1864, *Asia* became a floating barracks at Liverpool in 1867, and *Africa* was disposed of in the following year.

The competition between the Cunard and Collins vessels brought fares tumbling and freight rates dropped from £7 10s (£7·50) to £4 a ton. Records were made and broken and large sums of money wagered on the results of each voyage. Alarmed, the British Government requested Cunard to improve the mail service. The latter, game for a fight, wrote in 1853 to Viscount Canning, Postmaster General of the time :

> We can only retain our position on the Atlantic by continuing to build powerful ships. The risk of doing so is very great, as at the termination of a contract the ship would be valueless.

From this outlook the 3,300ton *Persia* was born in 1855. She was the first iron vessel of the Cunard Steamship Company Ltd and, in fact, the first iron paddle steamer on the Atlantic. Her hull was made of seven watertight compartments with 35ft iron keel bars and iron plates varying up to one inch thick. Side-lever engines of 950nhp were supplied and these had two cylinders 100·5in in diameter by 120in stroke which developed 3,600ihp and drove 38ft diameter paddle wheels to produce a normal speed of 13knots. Steam was supplied at 20psi from tubular box boilers of 26,080sq ft total heating surface in turn fired by 40 furnaces of 800sq ft grate area and burning 143tons of coal per day.

The year 1856 was to prove fateful for the Collins Line. Already one disaster had struck when, in September 1854, the *Arctic* was rammed by a small French steamer and sank with the loss of 322 lives, including Collins' wife, son, and daughter. In January 1856 *Pacific* and *Persia* left Liverpool at about the same time and a thrilling race appeared to be in prospect. In fact *Pacific* was never heard of again, while *Persia* limped into New York considerably overdue as a result of a collision with an iceberg which buckled her bow. The loss of *Pacific* was a great tragedy and the Collins Line never really recovered from it. A fifth vessel was launched in the April but she made only one voyage before the company collapsed as a result of its difficulties and a reduction in the subsidy. It was about this time that *Persia* made a crossing to New York in nine days, one hour and forty-five minutes to claim the Blue Riband which she was to hold for six years.

The second period in the history of steam passage across the Atlantic now starts to draw to a close and with it the use of paddle steamers on this route. In 1851 the Inman Line entered the lists with screw-driven vessels. This line aimed specifically at the emigrant trade which had been largely neglected by the steamer companies and which had been carried, often at very low fares, in the sailing ships of the Black Ball, Black Cross, White Diamond, and Red Cross companies. Until regulations were made in the forties requiring owners to provide bread and potatoes the unhappy passengers had risked disease and starvation if the voyage outlasted the provisions they had laid in store.

While the line only prospered for a short time, the Inman vessels made sufficient impact to sound the death knell for the paddle steamer opposition. The period became a racing period and there were casualties. There were also records, including, for example, a crossing from New York to Fastnet in seven days and twenty-three hours.

There was, however, one more fleet of paddle steamers to make a brief appearance on the scene and one more Cunard paddler to mention before the mail arrangements reverted to the Post Office and Cunard started operating screw-driven vessels. The company was the Atlantic Royal Mail Steam Navigation Company, later known as the Galway Line. Its first vessel was the 1,469ton *Pacific* built and engined by John Scott Russell & Co at Millwall. Two hundred and seventy feet long, *Pacific* had a clipper stem and a round stern with all but a few feet of parallel centre section built to Russell's 'wave-line' shaping. This two-funnelled vessel carried 80 first-class and 165 second-class passengers and had a speed of 14knots. She was sold as a blockade runner in 1861 and foundered off Cape Flattery thirteen years later.

The Galway Line had four more vessels, two built in 1860 by Palmers Shipbuilding & Iron Company of Jarrow and two built by Martin Samuelson & Company at Hull. The history of the line is a chapter of accidents. The service was due to start in June 1860 but *Connaught* was late in sailing from Galway and late in arriving at Boston. On her second trip she sprang a leak and then caught fire and had to be abandoned. *Columbia* was 360ft long and of 2,913 gross tons and was provided with eight water-tight compartments. An elegant and impressive vessel, she was, nevertheless, as unsuccessful as her sisters, taking seventeen days instead of seven on her maiden voyage. As a consequence of the accidents and delays to which the line seemed prone it was unable to fulfil the onerous speed obligations of the mail contract and was wound up.

Cunard's PS *Scotia* brought to an end a long line of paddle steamers and is a fitting vessel with which to conclude this portion of the paddle steamer story. *Scotia*, 379ft long and of 3,871 gross tons, had been intended to follow *Persia* in 1856 but was not launched until 1862. She was a well-proportioned vessel rigged as a two-masted brig and provided with two funnels rising from the promenade deck which stretched from stem to stern. Of immensely strong construction, some 2,800 tons of iron were used to fabricate her hull. Vessel and engines again came from

Napiers and cost £170,000. The engines were of the usual side-lever, jet-condensing type rated at 975nhp and having two 100in cylinders with a 12ft stroke.

What a sight those huge engines must have been as they drove the 40ft paddle wheels to move 240 passengers and 1,400 tons of cargo along at nearly 16knots. Even on her trials it was clear that the last Cunard paddler was a fast ship for she produced 15·31knots against a strong tide. No sooner had she shaken down than she took the eastbound Blue Riband from her consort *Persia* and in 1864 wrested the westbound record from the Collins Line. *Scotia* held the former honour until 1867 and the westbound laurels until 1869. Thus the paddler retired from the Atlantic in a blaze of glory, with *Scotia* the distinguished final representative of a worthy fleet of Cunard paddle steamers spanning a quarter of a century.

CHAPTER SEVEN

THE OTHER OCEANS

THE pattern of steamship development on the Atlantic routes was also apparent on the other oceans of the world. Here too, the carriage of mails was a significant factor with old companies expanding and new companies being formed, usually with the specific object of obtaining a mail contract. In most cases the new companies commenced their services by using paddle steamers although some of the later ones, like the General Screw Steam Shipping Company, owned no paddle vessels at all.

With the exception of the pioneer activities of bodies like the East India Company, progress and development tended to be slower and more difficult on the non-Atlantic routes largely due to the longer distances. It was impossible for the earlier vessels to carry sufficient coal for the long voyages and the more coal that had to be carried, the less space there was available for passengers and cargo. It was difficult to arrange re-fuelling points en route in the light of the availability of coal supplies and re-fuelling was a slow process which resulted in steamers losing the time advantage over their sailing vessel rivals.

There were two consequences of this situation which tended to retard the response of the steamer to the general pressure for improved communications. The first was the tendency for steam to develop in an ancillary rôle. By 1840 Green of Blackwall, for example, had a fleet of West Indiamen many of which had auxiliary steam power. Typical of the fleet was the *Earl of Hard-wicke*, a 1,600ton vessel in which only a space 24ft by 10ft was set aside for the engine. Of 30hp, this was designed to move the vessel when there was little wind and could produce a speed of five knots in calm weather.

The other consequence was that steam power did not come fully into its own until marine engines started to improve in efficiency thus affecting bunkering requirements and until the refinements of composite construction helped to improve the relationship between engine and bunkering space and that available for the payload. By this time screw propulsion was beginning to take over from the paddle and the main period of expansion thus depended more upon the former than the latter. Even so the contribution of the paddle steamer was not insignificant.

The Admiralty's reform of the Post Office packet service and the proposals that James MacQueen made in his 'General Plan for a Mail Communication between Great Britain and the Eastern and Western Parts of the World' influenced not only the mail arrangements on the Atlantic but also those for the West Indies. The Caribbean was at this time an important area in the eyes of the British Government and when MacQueen's Royal Mail Steam Packet Company secured the mail contract in March 1840, the subsidy amounted to £240,000 per year.

For the main routes of their new service the Royal Mail company ordered fourteen paddle steamers which were required by the contract to be of 450hp, to carry military personnel at reduced rates and to be capable of being fitted with the heaviest type of cannon. The size of the order resulted in it being shared among a number of shipyards, mainly on the Thames and Clyde. The vessels were all wooden paddlers but there were numerous differences in their features.

The first four vessels took up their Caribbean stations before the contract commenced. *Thames* sailed with passengers and mails from Gravesend on 29 December 1841 and *Tay* performed the maiden contract voyage two days later. The former called at Falmouth to pick up more mail on its outward voyage, but on the return journey sailed straight to Southampton. This period was one of considerable rivalry between the south coast ports with Falmouth anxious to retain its packet status and places like Plymouth, Dartmouth, and Portsmouth equally anxious to

THE OTHER OCEANS 77

acquire the privilege. In the end Southampton became the premier south coast port partly because of its railway facilities and partly because the Peninsular company shared the Royal Mail's preference.

All the early vessels of the Royal Mail Line carried the names of British rivers or estuaries. *Clyde*, the pioneer of the fleet, was built by R. Duncan & Company of Glasgow in 1841. She was a full-rigged vessel of 1,841 tons engined by Caird & Co with twin-cylinder simple engines which consumed 26 tons of coal per day in driving the 30ft paddles. In the line's first years of operation it lost six vessels and although *Clyde* was not one of them she did suffer the indignity of being stranded off Nevis in 1842. She was refloated then only to catch fire twelve years later and be broken up at St Thomas in the 1860s.

Another of the original Royal Mail vessels was the 1,940 ton *Forth* built by R. Menzies of Leith in 1841. She had three masts and a single funnel forward of the paddle boxes and, like her sisters, was constructed according to Admiralty specification with the government having the power to purchase at valuation. *Forth* foundered on the Alicranes reef off Yucatan in the Gulf of Mexico on 1 February 1849. The 1,800 ton *Tweed* had foundered on the same spot almost exactly two years earlier.

A passage time of nineteen days was the norm on the original main route from Falmouth (and then Southampton) to Barbados, but this steadily improved. The first revision of routes came with the transfer of mail handling to Southampton in 1843 and another major alteration with the revision of the mail contract in 1850. The new contract called for higher speeds and to meet this requirement the Royal Mail Line acquired four new paddle steamers and the displaced *Great Western*. Two of the new vessels had a short working life. *Amazon* was destroyed by fire in 1852, while *Orinoco* was scrapped in 1858 due to dry rot. With a sister vessel, *Demerara* being stranded on the way to have her engines fitted, this could not be considered a very successful class!

In addition to the misfortunes already mentioned, three of the original Royal Mail vessels had been lost in each of the years 1842, 1843, and 1844. The Line seemed to have more than its share of ill luck but despite this, the problems brought by the peculiar Caribbean weather, and the navigational hazards of opening up more direct routes than those used by the sailing vessels, the Royal Mail services continued to expand. Fresh ground was broken south of the Equator and the 1,700ton *Solent* of 1853 was followed by the company's first iron paddler, the 3,150ton *Atrato*. Three more paddle steamers, *Paramatta*, *Shannon*, and *Seine*, appeared in 1859 and 1860 before screw vessels took over completely.

The Pacific Steam Navigation Company, now a subsidiary of the Royal Mail Lines Ltd, has a long tradition of providing passenger and cargo services from Liverpool to the West Indies and the west coast of South America. The company dates back to 25 August 1835 when its founder, William Wheelwright, an enthusiastic believer in steam navigation as a way of opening up the Pacific coast of South America, obtained the exclusive rights of foreign navigation in Chilean ports and rivers. Other governments followed suit and, after failing to raise capital for his schemes in the United States, Wheelwright founded his company in London in 1839.

Wheelwright proposed to order two iron steamers of 700tons from Thomas Wilson, the Liverpool shipbuilder, at a cost of £9,000 each. Although the Liverpool shareholders were willing to become pioneers with iron steamers, the London shareholders were more cautious. They refused to agree to the order and thus wooden vessels were ordered instead. The result was the *Chile* which sailed from Falmouth in June 1840 to be followed by *Peru* in the following month. These vessels worked up and down the coast from Valparaiso to Panama receiving mails at the latter point after their journey via the Royal Mail Line and across the isthmus. Built of wood by Charles Young & Co of Limehouse, the two vessels were of 700tons gross register and were about 198ft long. Their 150hp engines were supplied by Miller & Ravenhill.

In its early years the Pacific Steam company nearly went bankrupt despite Wheelwright's energetic work in setting up repair facilities, finding coal supplies, and straightening out other problems. However, a mail contract in 1846 revived the line's fortunes. This contract seems to have been awarded more in the interests of British influence and commerce than for the benefit of the Exchequer since the receipts from the mails were very much less than the amount of the subsidy.

The Pacific Steam Navigation Company started to acquire iron paddle steamers from 1845 onwards, the vessels ranging in size from 373tons to 1,461tons and all bearing names associated with South America. Despite the special advantages of paddle steamers in the coastal work of the company's routes, the first screw vessel was introduced into the fleet in 1853 and the first steel vessel in 1860. In between, in 1856, came another milestone, two ironclad paddle steamers with compound reciprocating engines, *Inca* of 290tons and *Valparaiso* of 1,060tons. The company's final four paddle steamers were introduced in 1865.

The *Valparaiso* was fitted by John Elder with the first effective marine compound engine and, as such, was to make a tremendous impact on the shipping world. Although marine engine efficiency had previously been improving the resultant advantages had tended to be offset by rises in the price of coal. With all the complications of shipping coal out from England the dramatic economies produced by the Elder machinery were a godsend to the shipping business.

The energetic Wheelwright was promoted from chief superintendent to joint managing director in 1845 and built the business up to be the largest steamship company in the world with fifty-seven steamers and a total tonnage of 127,700tons by 1877. All was not plain sailing though, for of the eighty-seven vessels acquired between 1840 and 1877 seventeen were lost without trace, ten were shipwrecked, one capsized, and one was burned out. Wheelwright died in 1873 but the company continued to expand and modernise.

The P&O company started life with short sea services to the

Iberian Peninsular. The leading figures in the original firm, Brodie M'Gie Willcox and Arthur Anderson, had been London agents of the City of Dublin Steam Packet Company whose vessels they had been instrumental in chartering for use on behalf of the Spanish Government during the Spanish Civil War. At the end of the war came negotiations between Willcox and Anderson and the Irish company on the one hand and the Spanish Government on the other designed to establish good communications with England and out of these emerged the Peninsular Steam Navigation Company in 1835.

Most of the new company's vessels were obtained from the City of Dublin Steam Packet Company. One of these was the *William Fawcett*, a 206ton wooden paddler built in 1828 by Caleb Smith of Liverpool. *William Fawcett*, which had started life as a Mersey ferry and then worked on the London route, was not an ideal vessel for the rough weather which the Bay of Biscay can provide. She was powered by 60hp engines discharging their waste through a slender funnel of scarlet and black abaft the paddle boxes which rose high above the bulwarks. The other 1835 vessels were *City of Londonderry, Liverpool*, and *Royal Tar*. The latter was a 308ton paddler, 154ft long and with a beam of 27·7ft. Built in 1832, she had worked on charter to the Spanish Government and, as the *Reyna Governadera*, had landed men to resist the Carlist siege of Bilbao.

In 1836 the new company added *Braganza* to its fleet. She was three times the size of *William Fawcett* with a tonnage of 688tons and engines of 260hp. One year later came *Don Juan* and *Tagus*, both larger than *Braganza* and with engines of 286hp and 360hp respectively. By this time regular services were operating from London and Falmouth to Oporto, Lisbon, and Gibraltar.

The early years of the Peninsular company were not profitable ones and it set itself to obtain a mail contract. Based on the provision of five ships, the Peninsular's opening bid was £32,684. The rival Commercial Steam company's tender was £33,750. After a great deal of manoeuvring and Admiralty equivocation, the Peninsular Steam Navigation Company secured the contract and revived its tottering fortunes.

In 1840 the Admiralty sought tenders in connection with the carriage of the mails by sea to Egypt in substitution for the partially overland route across Europe. The Peninsular company bested three competitors for this and in September 1840 commenced the regular sailings stipulated in the £34,200 contract. At the same time the name was changed to the Peninsular & Oriental Steam Navigation Company and, after various amalgamations which included the absorption of the Trans-Atlantic Steamship Company, sailings east of Suez were also started. To operate the new service the vessels acquired from the Trans-Atlantic company, *Great Liverpool* and the 1,650ton *Oriental*, were used on the home section and two new vessels were built by Wilsons of Liverpool for the further section. The first of these was the two-funnel paddle steamer *Hindustan* which was sent out from Southampton in 1842. A year later she was followed by *Bentinck* which was also 217ft long and of 2,000tons. The latter was capable of two knots more than the *Hindustan*'s nine knots but she had something of a reputation as a coal eater. She was sold to the Calcutta Government in 1860.

In 1844 the P&O obtained a supplementary contract and added a Hong Kong route to the Calcutta service. Further contracts followed and eventually, as the East India Company's steamers became more and more semi-warships, the P&O became the Admiralty's sole mail contractor between Britain and the East. As the services expanded the company added further paddlers to its fleet until, in 1850 when the last new ones were put on the eastern section, fourteen such vessels were at work.

By this time a fairly stable operational situation existed with the Home Station, west of Suez, worked wholly by paddle steamers manned by white crews. East of Suez, known as the Eastern Station, the more exposed routes were the first to see screw vessels. Here there were two main legs, Suez–Calcutta and Bombay–Hong Kong with the vessels worked by Indian crews. By 1856 sailings had in most cases become fortnightly and the

P&O had reached Japan and Australia before the 1870s brought the end of its paddle steamer fleet and the new challenges brought by the opening of the Suez Canal.

The company's final small paddle steamer on the eastern section was the 600ton, 160ft *Pacha* which had been the P&O's first iron steamer when she started in the Peninsular trade in 1842. After being transferred from the Genoa service to the Calcutta–Hong Kong section in 1851 she sank with the loss of sixteen lives in the July of that year after colliding with *Erin* in the Malacca Strait. The last paddlers put to work west of Suez were *Valetta* and *Vectis* which worked from Marseilles to Alexandria from 1853 to 1865 and were then sold to the Egyptian Government, then *Delta* and *Massilia*—the former being the first British ship through the Suez Canal—and then, in 1863 and 1864, *Syria* and *Nyanza* which were eventually sold to the Union Line.

Before its retirement from the world's oceans the British paddle steamer had been seen in most foreign ports. Of those vessels which survived to displacement some became store ships or were converted to sail for the cheap conveyance of stores, others were sold to foreign owners to end their working lives in remote parts and on humble, but still useful, duties.

CHAPTER EIGHT

THE SECOND HALF OF THE CENTURY

THE years around the middle of the nineteenth century were exciting ones. Expanding commerce, growing prosperity and the gold rushes in California and Australia all added to the need for improved sea communications. Despite the impetus of steam propulsion a generation of sailing vessels, developed out of the famed opium clippers, held their own until the opening of the Suez Canal in 1869, combined with improvements in marine engine design, ended their graceful era.

The Baltimore clippers with their sleek hulls easily outpaced the blunt-bowed, stubby East Indiamen and produced some remarkable journey times. In 1850 the clipper *Oriental* reached the Thames only ninety-seven days after leaving Hong Kong and with their home ports freed from restriction and the demand for tea rising, British shipowners and builders were forced to look to their laurels. Firms such as Halls of Aberdeen rose to the occasion, while the Thames-side yards steadily improved on the design of the Blackwall frigates which spanned thirty-eight years and carried many thousands to the developing colonies.

The year 1866 was notable. Not only was it the year of the famous China tea clipper race when *Taeping* narrowly beat *Ariel* by being the first of the two to secure a tug for the last leg of the journey to London, but for the first time steam tonnage exceeded the tonnage under sail. Steam powered shipping had, in fact, been growing much faster than sail for some time. Between 1840 and 1849 British sailing tonnage increased by 23·5 per cent and steam tonnage by 81 per cent while between 1850 and 1859 the increases were 26·5 per cent and 184 per cent respectively.

The middle of the century was notable for the amount of change which took place in the statute book as it affected merchant shipping. The process started in 1849 with the repeal of the navigation laws which had kept British ports closed to foreign competition for two centuries, a move that aroused bitter opposition from shipowners many of whom sold their businesses. In 1854 the coasting trade was also freed from protection. This was also the year, not only of the declaration of war upon Russia, but of the Merchant Shipping Act which dealt with officers, pilotage, wrecks, measurement, and registration. For the first time masters and chief mates were required to have certificates of competence.

Prior to the 1854 Act, the measurement of vessels was based on the original wine 'tun' and was calculated by multiplying the keel, breadth, and depth measurements and dividing the product by ninety-four. After the Act, gross tonnage represented internal capacity based on one hundred cubic feet to the ton with net tonnage being this figure less non-earning space such as that taken up by the machinery and crews' quarters.

In addition to the 1854 Act, statutes of 1852 and 1855 dealt with the unsatisfactory conditions under which emigrants had previously been carried. An Act of 1862 introduced improved rules of navigation and required steamers of over 100nhp to have two certificated engineers. Subsequent regulations in the 1860s and 1870s dealt further with conditions on merchant vessels, their seaworthiness and like matters.

The years from 1850 to 1875 not only covered the decline of the American clipper and the evolution of shipping regulations, but also embraced the replacement of the paddle by screw propulsion on the high seas. The P&O's last paddler was converted to screw propulsion in 1874 and Cunard's magnificent *Scotia* was put into reserve two years later and then converted to a twin-screw vessel. The early problems of screw propulsion were overcome and, with the advent of the more reliable twin-screw vessels and compound engines with their considerable economies in fuel and space, the paddle steamer bowed out from

Page 85: (above) An elegant and impressive liner of the Galway Line the 2,913ton PS *Columbia*; (below) the Royal Mail Steam Packet Company made Southampton its home port and this scene in Southampton Water is typical of the early years

Page 86: *(above)* This scene from the north shows MacBrayne's PS *Iona* at North Pier, Oban; *(below)* further south the Bristol Steam Navigation Company's PS *Juno* passes through the Avon Gorge

the world of deep-sea shipping. In the same process of evolution wooden vessels gave way to ships of composite construction and then to iron vessels and the familiar sailing rig began to lose its auxiliary role and disappear altogether.

Despite the decline of the paddle steamer on the high seas during the second half of the century, this form of shipping continued to develop and expand for some time longer in the estuaries and on the coastal and short sea routes. Major companies, like GSN, continued to take delivery of paddle steamers. At the same time the population, which had doubled in the first half of the century, continued to grow, while the gradual increase in wealth and leisure brought with it not only a need for constantly improving sea communications but also a greater demand for entertainment, including sea and river trips.

Many of the early steamers had a good long life which took them into the second fifty years of the century. GSN's 393ton *Columbine*, for example, had been built at Deptford in 1826 and worked a variety of routes before she was stranded near Rotterdam in 1855. At the same time a new generation of steamers became necessary for the expanding cargo trade and to provide faster passenger services both to keep abreast of competition and to give the excursion passenger a day trip with a worthwhile period on shore. Not only were larger and faster vessels required, but the public demanded a higher standard of comfort and amenity.

Between 1850 and 1873 GSN took delivery of thirty-five new paddle steamers, twenty-one of them in the 1850s. Then, in 1875, came the firm's last three iron paddlers, *Atlas, Swallow*, and *Swift*. A period of screw vessels followed until, in 1887, the first of a new group of 17knot steel paddle steamers was delivered from J. Scott & Company of Kingston. These vessels were used by the company to open up a new service to Yarmouth. All had saloon decks extending the width of the vessel and carried forward of the paddle boxes.

GSN's last cargo paddle vessel, *Taurus*, was built in 1866 for the Continental cattle trade. This steamer was fitted to carry 650

F

cattle and 500 sheep and had a cruising speed of about 14knots. She worked between Tonning and Hamburg and between Antwerp/Geestemunde and London until 1892 by which time the cattle trade had diminished considerably.

An important event in the second half of the century was the introduction of the name of David MacBrayne to the shipping scene, first as a partner in David Hutcheson & Co which took over the West Highland business of G. & J. Burns and then, from 1879, as principal of the shipping company which still bears his name. The company's first new vessel PS *Mountaineer* (I) vastly improved the Ardrishaig route but misfortune struck three subsequent vessels, *Chevalier* (I) (1853) and the first two *Iona*s. The third *Iona*, launched in May 1854, lorded the Ardrishaig route until the Glasgow and Inveraray Steamboat Company's *Lord of the Isles* appeared in 1877, an event which led to the building of the famous *Columba*.

MacBraynes continued to introduce new paddle steamers up to 1910 when the third *Mountaineer* was launched by A. & J. Inglis Ltd. The network of routes extended northwards from the Clyde embracing the Western Isles and the Caledonian Canal. The developing railway network affected the pattern of the services but brought more users especially in the summer when the mails, the local travellers, and their goods were swelled by increasing numbers of holidaymakers. Many notable paddlers worked from places like Inverness, Oban, Corpach, Tobermory and the Clyde and it was a sad day when *Pioneer* (II) retired from the fleet in 1944 to end this long tradition.

On the Irish Sea the Isle of Man Steam Packet Company continued to take delivery of new paddle steamers with *Mona's Queen* (I) in 1852 and *Douglas* (I) in 1858. About this time the straight stem began to replace clipper bows and *Mona's Isle* (II) was the first of the company's paddlers in the new style and the first to be fitted with oscillating engines. After twenty-three years she was converted to screw operation and then tragically lost in a fierce gale in the Mersey in 1909. Six more twin-funnelled paddlers followed.

In 1878 the company took delivery of its first screw vessels. However, it had by no means finished with paddlers and purchased from Caird & Company its longest, fastest, and most luxurious vessel, the 1,564ton *Mona's Isle* (III). Next came the 1,559ton *Mona's Queen* which brought the time for the crossing from Liverpool down to three hours, thirty-five minutes. In 1888 *Queen Victoria* and *Prince of Wales* were added to the fleet to be followed by *Tynwald* (III) and *Empress Queen*. The latter, of 1,995tons and fitted with diagonal, three-crank, compound engines developing 10,000ihp, was one of the largest and fastest paddle steamers of her day and was capable of just over 21·5knots.

The first round of competition in this period came from rival companies based at Ramsey and Castletown and operating *Manx Fairy* and *Ethel Vannin* respectively. Until the latter was sold in 1858 to the Sardinian Government for £4,070 there were some exciting races between these vessels and their main rivals, *Mona's Queen* and *Countess of Ellesmere*.

The second period of competition started in 1887 with the Isle of Man, Liverpool & Manchester Steam Ship Company (the Manx Line) using *Queen Victoria* and *Prince of Wales* and the Isle of Man Steam Navigation Company (the Lancashire Line) using *Lancashire Witch*. The latter was a slow vessel but *Prince of Wales* on one occasion covered the distance from Liverpool to Douglas in three hours. Competition from the Manx Line led to the usual round of fare reductions and only ceased when the Isle of Man Steam Packet Company bought out its rival.

In 1895 *Lady Tyler* of the Mutual Line of Manx Steamers Ltd operated for three months on the route but proved too slow and her owners went bankrupt. Then came a Mr Higginbottom trading as Liverpool & Douglas Steamers Ltd. His attempt to purchase two ex-Holyhead to Kingstown vessels was thwarted by the Manx company but eventually the new rival placed the old *Ireland* on the route and followed this with the acquisition of two railway paddle steamers from the Newhaven to Dieppe route.

The ex-LNWR vessels *Lily* and *Violet* were fairly successful and so was the *Calais-Douvres* but the company lost money and collapsed when Mr Higginbottom died in 1902.

Paddle steamers lasted longer on some Irish Sea routes than on others. The Belfast Steamship Company came into being in January 1852 as a result of the merchants of Belfast becoming uneasy at the prospect of being at the mercy of the competing companies providing services to Liverpool. Eighteen months after its inception the new company placed the notable *Telegraph* on the route and later the 206ft *Sea Nymph*, but then acquired its first screw vessel and disposed of the two paddlers to the Chester & Holyhead Railway. A later paddler, the *William McCormick*, was taken over with the Londonderry Steamboat Company Ltd, but she was sold and converted to a sailing ship.

A fine paddle steamer on the Bristol Steam Navigation Company's service between Bristol and Cork was the two-funnelled iron vessel *Juno* which was placed on the route in 1868. Built by the London & Glasgow Engineering & Iron Shipbuilding Company and of 1,019tons, *Juno* remained on the Cork route until the Bristol company sold this to the City of Cork Steam Packet Company in 1900. Further north a complex of local routes operated in the Morecambe–Blackpool and Liverpool–Llandudno areas. Both typified the period with small fleets carrying long titles and single-vessel concerns changing ownership fairly often, but imperceptibly giving way to fewer operators and more stable services.

In the English Channel after seventeen years of operating the mail service the Admiralty gave up the work in favour of Jenkins & Churchward of Dover who traded as the English, French & Belgian Royal Mail Company. Four vessels were taken over with the work, but *Undine* was sold to the *Morning Herald* for carrying news dispatches and *Violet* was wrecked on the Goodwins with considerable loss of life. Replacement vessels were introduced during the 1850s including the two-funnel, 340ton *John Penn* from Thames Ironworks in 1859. This vessel made a record crossing from Dover to Calais of one hour, twenty-three minutes in its first year of operation. For many years Jenkins & Churchward, together with the South Eastern Railway, carried most of the cross-channel traffic.

Standing between the short sea trade and the excursion business came the other functional routes and the services which fulfilled both communication and pleasure functions. An example of the former was the service from Penzance to the Isles of Scilly which started on a regular basis in 1858 with the 480ton *Scotia*. A good example of the latter was the network of services in the Bristol Channel where several companies and a variety of vessels linked points on the Welsh and English coasts with voyages as far afield as Hayle and Lundy Island.

The second half of the century was a gay time for the coastal excursion trade with new companies constantly appearing and amalgamations gradually shaping the ultimate survivors. Competition was keen. On the south coast in 1876, for example, three companies competed for the Weymouth–Swanage–Bournemouth traffic, while *Royal Saxon* brought the return fare on the Isle of Wight run down to $4\frac{1}{2}$d for a short period. It was about this time that Cosens introduced the 173ton *Empress* which was to remain in service for over seventy-five years. The 160·1ft long *Empress* was built of iron in 1879 by Samuda Bros and had vertical oscillating engines by J. Penn & Son, Greenwich. She had low paddle boxes and the bridge forward of the funnel and was specially strengthened at the bows to nose onto the steeply shelving shore at places like Lulworth Cove. In the same period the Southampton company introduced a family of iron paddle steamers from Barclay, Curle & Company. Starting with *Southampton* in 1872, these vessels had a single funnel forward of the paddles, compound diagonal engines, an open foredeck, and a narrow saloon aft.

All the popular holiday areas had their excursion fleets and although screw vessels became more numerous, paddle steamers continued to operate all round our coast. The pleasure trade was frequently combined with other work and the South West provided many examples of this, of numerous owners operating in one area and also of the way so many ex-railway vessels found a new lease of life.

The south coasts of Devon and Cornwall also had their share of paddle steamer operations. Companies like the Fowey & Par Steamship Company provided regular services between these two ports with the 87ton *Forager* and then the 181ton *Albatross*, both built in Hull and acquired from Norfolk owners. At Falmouth the packet services to places like Truro had become the province of screw steamers by 1850, but diminutive paddlers ranging from the 49ton *Duke of Buccleugh* of 1830 to the 73ton *Pendennis* of 1863 spent many years doing passenger work in the summer and towing in the winter. At Plymouth William Gilbert gradually emerged as the dominant figure in a very competitive scene and by 1892 had a fleet of three screw and five paddle vessels. On the Dart, where paddle steamer operation dates back to 1836, the present company originated with paddle steamers like the 101ton *Pilot* from South Shields and the 104ton *Guide* from Hayle. Then came the noted 'Castle' paddlers commencing with the 73ton *Berry Castle* built at Kingswear in 1880.

Further east, at Exmouth, the docks had been authorised by an Act of 1864 to overcome the need to transfer traffic from schooners to lighters. In 1891 the Devon Dock, Pier & Steamship Company ordered the paddler *Duchess of Devonshire* for a cost of £12,000 and three years later acquired a sister vessel, *Duke of Devonshire*. This famous pair served the area for many years, long enough for their crews to develop a special expertise in canting their ships to negotiate the narrow entrance to the dock.

The second half of the century produced very different situations on the Thames and Clyde largely because the expanding railway services were competitive on the former and complementary in the latter case. As railways extended along both sides of the Thames estuary the steamers progressively came to rely more and more on excursion traffic.

In 1876 the London Steamboat Company Ltd emerged with a fleet of seventy vessels from various amalgamations of the Iron,

Citizen, London and Westminster, Waterman, and Woolwich companies. In an attempt to retain some of the local traffic the new company operated a half-hourly, all the year round service between Chelsea and Greenwich and Woolwich, but although fares were cheap passengers lost their taste for exposing themselves to wintry conditions and the business became more and more seasonal.

Matters worsened after the *Princess Alice* disaster in 1878 and the company sold out in 1884. With traffic declining and capital in short supply succeeding operators fared no better. A bad season meant foreclosure of mortgages on the vessels and in 1887 the River Thames Steamboat Company owed so much in unpaid dues at Clacton that the pier company banned the landing of passengers there. This lost the resort some 25,000 passengers annually and led to the formation of the London, Woolwich and Clacton-on-Sea Steamboat Company Ltd which later became Belle Steamers Ltd. In the same year, 1888, GSN with its wider interests managed to declare a dividend of 3s 9d (19p) per share for the previous year.

A final effort to revive the local business, a ten-minute steamer service between Chelsea and London Bridge at very low fares, failed to attract business in face of the competition with the London General Omnibus and London Road Car companies. After this steamer services only carried excursion business and this started to pick up at the beginning of the 1890s when the new breed of paddle steamers like *Koh-i-Noor* carried many thousands to places like Margate and the increasingly popular Continental resorts.

The original single-funnel Thames paddle steamers had been highly ornamental and the annual parade of City steamboats at Chelsea was a pageant of colour. Later the excursion vessels steadily became larger and more functional while the local services were often operated by paddlers resembling overgrown lifeboats whose only enlivening features were the enamel signs on their sponsons. Typical of these was the diminutive *Warrior*. A few vessels had two funnels like the wooden Watkins steamer

Uncle Sam built at Poplar in 1849 by R. H. Green. After ten years on the Mersey towing sailing vessels *Uncle Sam* returned to the Thames for a mixture of towing, salvage, and guest boat work and lasted until 1900.

The 1860s were stirring years on the Clyde with forty-three new steamers entering the fierce competition for traffic. Among these was *Undine*, the first vessel to be fitted with a single diagonal engine and a Scotch boiler, and, in 1865, the 156·51ton *Sultana* which frequently beat her rivals to Princes Pier, Greenock and the waiting Glasgow train. Her efforts resulted in her skipper being fined on more than one occasion.

The pace began to slow down with the loss of good vessels to the American theatre of war and the growing power of the railways, especially the newly opened Wemyss Bay Railway and its associated steamboat company, to dictate terms. The slower pace shows up in the fact that only eighteen steamers were launched in the 1870s.

Further bouts of competition took place in the last twenty years of the century but these were not aired outside Scotland. The national advertisements of the rival railways laid more stress on the merits of their routes and facilities than on their local steamer connections but even so the steamer rivalry began to affect the popularity of the Clyde resorts and the century ended on a note of greater co-operation.

CHAPTER NINE

THE RÔLE OF THE RAILWAYS

RAILWAYS appeared on the scene less than twenty-five years after the first British commercial paddle steamer. As the expanding network of lines developed it took most of the freight business from the canals and much of the passenger traffic from the coastal steamers. Where they could not compete, the traffic-hungry railways showed themselves anxious to form links with steamer routes, especially if a rival company appeared to be interested.

The enabling Acts of the railway companies did not normally include powers to operate steamers and the initial forms of co-ordination involved linking train services with privately operated steamers. This rarely proved completely satisfactory and the railways rapidly sought more effective control, at first by operating through subsidiaries and later by obtaining their own powers.

The first examples of rail and steamer routes were provided by the London & Blackwall Railway on the Thames and the Glasgow, Paisley & Greenock Railway on the Clyde. In the sphere of deep-sea operation the London & South Western Railway was interested in steamers as early as 1845 when the South Western Steam Packet Company was established. Sponsored by the railway, this company was formed from the South of England Steam Nagivation and the British & Foreign Steam Navigation companies which had operated services between Southampton, Jersey, St Malo, and Granville. The L&SW obtained its own powers in 1848 and operated its own steamers from 1849, finally absorbing its shipping subsidiary in 1862.

The early South Western steamers were mainly of iron and from the yards of Ditchburn & Mare. In 1863 and 1864 the first wholly owned railway steamers were introduced to stimulate business to and from the Channel Islands. Two-funnelled and with oscillating engines producing some 15·5knots the first of these, *Normandy*, was lost in a collision in March 1870. The second, *Brittany*, lasted much longer. After being enlarged in 1873 and re-engined in 1883 she worked between Southampton and Havre until finally broken up in 1900.

From 1867 the Jersey–St Malo–Granville service was worked by the paddler *Granville*, an erstwhile rival on the route purchased from the French. This was a period of intense competition for the cross-Channel business, each railway to the south coast pressing the advantages of its route on potential customers and seeking to reduce the journey time to the various French destinations. To improve passage times the L&SW introduced two fast ex-blockade runners and then, in 1871, came the final cross-Channel paddle steamer *Wolf* which worked between Southampton and Cherbourg for thirty-one years.

With the take-over of the Lymington Railway and the Solent Steam Ship Company in 1884, the L&SW acquired two old paddlers, *Solent* and *Mayflower*. A new steel paddler, *Lymington*, was introduced in 1893 and in 1902 a new *Solent* replaced the older vessel of that name. These vessels worked to Totland Bay and Alum Bay as well as running the Yarmouth service.

The South Eastern Railway reached Ashford in 1842 and until the extension to Dover two years later, passengers and mails were carried forward by coach. From 1843 the railway passengers, by arrangement with the New Commercial Steam Packet Company, completed their journey across the Channel by using the three steamers *William Wallace, Emerald*, and *City of Boulogne* operating between Folkestone and Boulogne. As the traffic expanded the SER formed its own steamer subsidiary, the South Eastern & Continental Steam Packet Company, which operated from Dover to Calais, Ostend, and Boulogne and from Folkestone to Boulogne with four vessels from Ditchburn & Mare and four from Lairds. In 1853 the SER took over direct operation from its subsidiary.

Several notable vessels were operated by the SER before its

amalgamation with the London, Chatham & Dover Railway in 1899. These included the *Napoleon III* from Samuda Bros in 1865—the first cross-Channel steamer with a boat deck—and the company's first steel ships *Albert Victor* and *Louise Dagmar*. The latter were fitted with bow rudders to enable them to turn in the confines of Boulogne Harbour. *Louise Dagmar* was damaged in a collision in 1893, the year in which *Albert Edward* ran on the rocks near Cap Gris Nez, filled as the tide rose and had to be abandoned as a total loss.

By the time *Mabel Grace*, the last cross-Channel paddle steamer, was commissioned in 1899, large, fast paddle steamers were not exceptional. *Mabel Grace* herself was of 1,215tons and had a speed of over twenty knots. She was a handsome vessel, but then most of the SER paddlers were good-looking ships with black hulls and white upper works, including white funnels with a black, bell-mouth top. The house flag was blue with the letters SER in white.

In 1861 the London, Chatham & Dover Railway reached Dover and challenged the SER Folkestone route to France by acquiring the Dover–Calais mail contract from Jenkins & Churchward. Until it obtained its own powers in 1864 the railway used the displaced contractor's vessels to maintain the service. Some of these, in fact, continued at work when the LC&D started operating in its own right, among them *Samphire* which was rammed by a badly lit American sailing barge during haze in 1865. *Samphire* was severely damaged and only some of the passengers were rescued by the Ostend mail steamer *Belgique*. Fortunately the bulkheads held and *Samphire* was subsequently repaired.

After the gallant but unsuccessful attempt to conquer the effect of the rough seas of the English Channel with three paddlers of unusual design, the LC&D introduced four new, trim, double-ended craft with twin funnels and well-raked masts. The first was the popular, electrically lit *Invicta* from the Thames Ironworks in 1882. Then, between 1886 and 1889, came three vessels from Fairfields, *Victoria* (I), which once made a crossing in sixty minutes, *Empress* (I) of 1,123tons and 20·5knots, and the 1,212ton *Calais-Douvres* (II) built to stimulate the Paris Exhibition traffic. Both *Invicta* and *Empress* once suffered the indignity of having their passengers taken off by carts, the former when she was stranded on the French coast in 1882 and the latter after she had broken a paddle wheel on the pierhead at Calais. The LC&D vessels and the marine department which operated them enjoyed a first-class reputation, but the day of the turbine and the screw meant that no more paddle steamers would be built after the two railways combined to form the South Eastern & Chatham Railway.

The other Southern Railway constituent, the London, Brighton & South Coast Railway, did not fare too well in its early steamer activities.

Inheriting part of a traditional link to France via Dieppe, the railway ran into trouble first with the rival claims of Brighton, Shoreham, and Newhaven to be the English terminal and then with the SER which exposed the 'Brighton's' investment in the Brighton & Continental Steam Packet Company at a time when the railway had no powers to own vessels. When Maple & Morris took over the service on contract using old G. & J. Burns' vessels it had little reputation for anything but cheapness, facilities both on the vessels and at Newhaven being quite inadequate for the numbers which the low fares attracted. Matters did, however, improve particularly when the LB&SC obtained its own powers to operate. The main routes were from Newhaven to Dieppe in conjunction with the Western Railway of France and from Littlehampton and to Jersey and St Malo.

In the year of the 1878 Paris Exhibition the eight paddle steamers of the LB&SCR carried 146,751 passengers. Two of these vessels, the 221ft *Brighton* and *Victoria*, had been specially ordered from John Elder of Govan for the event. Engines by the Brighton Company's renowned Locomotive & Marine Superintendent, William Stroudley, drove 17ft paddle wheels and produced a speed of 16knots. Four years later came *Brittany* and *Normandy*. These 231ft vessels were fitted with Stroudley's feathering paddles comprising nine curved steel floats with a heavy paddle arm but no outer rim.

The LB&SC steamers had black hulls, white above the strake and with white paddle boxes. The house flag consisted of the cross of St George with alternate corners of blue and red. No 'Brighton' steamer was ever fitted with a bridge but the 1822 pair had a three-sided shelter at the forward end of the promenade deck.

Normandy once made a crossing in three hours and thirty-two minutes and this record lasted for three years. It fell in 1888 to the two vessels designed by William Stroudley for the 1889 Paris Exhibition traffic. In the September of that year *Paris* made the crossing in three hours and twenty-five minutes, only to have *Rouen* beat this by five minutes the very next day. These two vessels were 250ft long and had two black and white topped funnels 7ft in diameter and set rakishly at an angle of thirteen degrees.

In 1880 the L&SW and the LB&SC jointly purchased the private steamers operating between Portsmouth and the Isle of Wight. A double-ended paddler, *Victoria*, worked the service and then in 1884 two further such vessels, *Duchess of Edinburgh* and *Duchess of Connaught*, were introduced. Both had two funnels athwartship and both were extremely ugly. Other paddle steamers followed to produce a railway paddler tradition on this route of over ninety years.

In the North West railway steamers appeared on the scene when the Chester & Holyhead Railway completed its line along the traditional stage coach route to Ireland. The steamer service on from Holyhead to Kingstown was operated by the paddle steamers *Anglia, Hibernia, Scotia,* and *Cambria.* They were joined by the cargo vessels *Ocean* and *Hercules* in 1852, while six years later the railway was absorbed by the growing London & North Western Railway.

In 1860 the Irish mail contract passed to the City of Dublin Steam Packet Company who used *Ulster, Munster, Leinster,* and *Connaught* on the work until three years before the end of the century. Despite this competition, the L&NW continued to expand its activities, particularly in the cargo sphere. In 1863 a new service was introduced between Holyhead and Dublin (North Wall) with sailings from Holyhead at 1pm and 4pm and from Dublin at noon and 9pm. Other major events on the route included a new express service for the growing passenger trade. The new schedules commenced in 1876 and utilised two large, fast paddlers from Lairds of Birkenhead who also built the 1,035ton *Lily* and *Violet* which operated the night express service introduced in 1880.

Four paddle steamers worked on the LNW's Greenore route starting in 1873 with the 917ton *Eleanor* built by R. Stephenson & Company of Newcastle. Her opposite number was the Dublin-built *Countess of Erne*. Neither steamer lasted until the route was taken over by screw vessels in 1895, *Eleanor* being stranded on Leestone Point, Co Down in 1881 and *Countess of Erne* finishing up as a coal hulk. The LNWR also operated paddle ferries across the Mersey prior to the opening of Birkenhead Woodside as well as a paddle tug between Ellesmere Port and Liverpool.

The Midland Railway came into the steamer world when it acquired the 'Little' North Western Railway and access to Morecambe in 1859. Association with the Furness Railway, whose steamer powers were confined to a Morecambe–Barrow service, and James Little & Company of Belfast led to the formation in 1867 of the Barrow Steam Navigation Company and to the inauguration of steamer services from Morecambe to Belfast and Barrow to Douglas. The paddle steamers used ranged in size from the 221·6ft, 446ton *Herald* of 1866 to the 278·9ft, 989ton *Manx Queen* of 1882.

The steady trend of increasing trade and pleasure travel demanded more and more rail-ship links. To meet this need an Act of Parliament was obtained in 1870 authorising Fleetwood–Belfast/Londonderry services by the L&Y and LNW railways who took over the North Lancashire Steam Navigation Company and introduced four more paddle steamers. The mainstays of this route were five sizeable vessels starting with the Tyne-built *Prin-*

cess of Wales and ending with the 1,429ton *Prince of Wales*, the last paddle steamer on the route. In 1902 the L&Y acquired the Liverpool, Fleetwood, and Drogheda services of the Drogheda Steam Packet Company together with its paddle steamers.

The constituents of the London Midland & Scottish Railway operated other paddle steamers and services than those mentioned above. The LT&SR, for example, used paddle steamers on its Tilbury–Gravesend ferry service while a number of paddle tugs were in use in connection with the extensive ancillary activities that stemmed from these wide shipping and harbour interests. Perhaps the most attractive house flag was that of the Midland Railway which depicted a red wyvern on a white background.

The Great Western Railway, of course, had an early connection with paddle steamers through Brunel. As with the other companies its first steamer links were on an agency basis but even when it took over direct responsibility the GWR never achieved the same reputation for its marine services as the main railway operations enjoyed. Although GWR steamer ownership did not start until 1872, the railway had acquired two wooden paddle tugs when it took over the Shrewsbury & Chester Railway in 1854 and it is interesting to note that in September 1859 the GWR was offering excursion facilities to view the *Great Eastern* at Weymouth. The results were as disappointing as the career of that mammoth vessel.

On the Weymouth–Channel Islands route, the Great Western's own services were inaugurated with screw vessels, but prior to the railway taking over in 1889 the Weymouth & Channel Islands Steam Packet Company had operated paddle steamers including the ex LB&SC vessel *Brighton*. On the New Milford–Waterford service the GWR took over from its agents Ford & Jackson in 1872 and quickly obtained new tonnage including three single-funnel paddlers from Simons of Renfrew. In 1880 came the Great Western's first steel vessel, the handsome 254ft *Pembroke* from Lairds, which was converted to twin-screw propulsion in 1895–6 and then lasted until 1925 after having been transferred to the Channel Islands service in 1915.

Steamer services on the Severn New Passage Ferry started in 1825. When the railway to Black Rock and from New Passage village was completed in 1863 the 100ton paddler *Gem* and the 163ton *Relief* were taken over to form the link between the two lines. The 1839 paddle tug *President* by Thomas Raffield of Birkenhead was purchased in 1863 and the 159ton *Christopher Thomas* in 1864. The GWR added the 188ton *Chepstow* in 1875 but the ferry fell into disuse for a time after the opening of the Severn Tunnel and paddle steamers were not used again.

Millbay Docks at Plymouth were acquired by the railway interests in 1846. The ocean trade took a long while to build up but by the 1870s tenders had become a necessity and the 173ton iron paddler *Sir Francis Drake* was acquired from William Allsup of Preston to meet this demand. The GWR also owned a number of other small paddle vessels at one time or another, ranging from the two tugs taken over with the Bristol & Exeter Railway to excursion vessels on the Salcombe river.

On the east coast the Great Eastern Railway came into being in 1862, taking over the Eastern Counties Railway and the Eastern Union Railway and acquiring the eight-year-old line to Harwich. Regular railway steamer services to Rotterdam superseded the charter vessel arrangements with the advent of the iron paddle steamer *Zealous* from J. & W. Dudgeon in 1864. Then came the two-funnel *Avalon* from the same builders in 1865. The first channel packet to have a straight rather than clipper stern, *Avalon* was fitted with two-cylinder simple oscillating engines which gave her a speed of 14 knots.

In 1871 came the 239·8ft *Richard Young*, the first vessel to pass through the new Hook of Holland waterway, and then the elegant *Claud Hamilton*, a 962-ton paddler named after the chairman of the company. After 1897 this vessel worked for the Corporation of London ferrying cattle from Deptford to the foreign cattle boats at Gravesend. The first GER steel paddler and the last paddle vessel to be used on Continental services was the rakish *Adelaide*, but the railway operated a variety of smaller

Page 103: (above) The London & South Western Railway steamers PS *Brittany* (1864–1900) and *Cherbourg*; (below) Simons & Company of Renfrew built the PS *Waterford* (1874–1905) for the Great Western Railway

Page 104: *(above)* The famous Navy trials between the screw of HMS *Rattler* and the paddles of HMS *Alecto* in 1845; *(below)* a much later naval paddle vessel, the Ascot class minesweeper HMS *Atherstone*, later PS *Queen of Kent*

paddlers for towing, ferry, and excursion work on the Thames, the Orwell, and at Lowestoft.

Farther north a number of railway paddle steamers operated in and from the Humber estuary. The railway ferry service operated under an Act of Parliament entitled 'Steam Communications across the Humber Act 1846' and started with two small vessels *Falcon* and *Magna*. These were followed by *Queen* and *Prince of Wales* purchased from the Greenwich Steam Packet Company for £2,300. For its later ferry vessels the Manchester, Sheffield & Lincolnshire Railway took the names of the towns it served with the 220ton *Liverpool* and the 216ton *Doncaster* from Samuelsons and the 221ton *Manchester* from the Goole Shipbuilding & Engineering Company. From 1865 the MS&L operated short sea services while continuing the paddle steamer tradition on the ferry with successive paddle steamers bearing the names of local towns.

An example of the steamer services operated by the smaller companies is the Lough Swilly services. Originally the railway had arrangements with various charter steamers and trains connected with the paddlers *Vista, Swilly*, and *Alexandra*. When train services on the Lough Swilly branch ceased in 1865, *Swilly* suffered the indignity of being left to rot on the beach. She had been built in Hull in 1849, and was 82ft long.

From 1877 the Lough Swilly Steamship Company worked the services until the Londonderry & Lough Swilly Railway took over again in 1923. The last paddlers on the lough were the stubby 90ton *Kate* which worked from 1869 to 1912 and the 140ton *Lake of Shadows* which, despite a stranding while working a Sunday excursion in 1923, lasted until 1934. Other Irish railways operating paddle steamers included the Belfast & County Down Railway, the Great Southern & Western Railway, the Sligo, Leitrim & Northern Counties Railway, and various smaller lines.

Another minor railway to operate paddle steamers was the Somerset & Dorset and its predecessors. From the opening of the Somerset Central Railway's Burnham extension in May 1858

G

steamers operated between Burnham and Cardiff more or less regularly until 1888. In addition to passengers, dairy produce was carried to South Wales and rails brought back. The first regular vessel was the *Taliesin* of the Cardiff Steam Navigation Company with the railway paddler *Ruby* following in 1860. Various other paddle vessels operated during the years 1863 to 1884 when the two-funnelled PS *Sherbro* took over for four years before being sold to Spanish owners. As part of its short-lived project for a route from South Wales to France in conjunction with the L&SW, the S&D chartered the 307ton paddler *Albion* to work to Cherbourg in 1865 and 1866.

The extensive steamer business down the Clyde was bound to attract the interest of early Scottish railway promoters and, not unnaturally, the advent of rail and steamer links via Gourock brought a fresh wave of competition to the area. The two attempts by the railway to operate their own services were not successful and an uneasy peace, based on the private steamers carrying passengers forward from Custom House Quay at Greenock, lasted until 1865. In that and the following year several new factors arose. First the Caledonian Railway obtained a new outlet to the coast via the Wemyss Bay Railway and then came new challenges through the authorisation of the Glasgow & South Western Railway's better route via Albert Harbour at Greenock and the North British Railway obtaining access to Helensburgh.

The challenge of the G&SW through Albert Harbour and of the NBR through Helensburgh, and later Craigendoran, made the Caledonian Railway revive its plans for new facilities at Gourock and, failing to secure co-operation from the private steamers, to form the Caledonian Steam Packet Company with Captain Williamson of the *Sultana* as marine superintendent. Racing was widespread, with trains being given a clear run on the rival routes and the passengers hustled onto the waiting steamers with scant ceremony. Typical of the regular competitors were the G&SW's *Minerva* under Captain Archibald Henderson and the Caley's *Galatea* commanded by Captain Duncan Bell.

With the acquisition of the Lanarkshire & Ayrshire Railway the Caledonian companies made a bid for the Arran traffic by introducing the renowned *Duchess of Hamilton* which earned her builders, Denny of Dumbarton, a premium by exceeding her contract speed of 18knots during her trials. The G&SW replied with the two-funnel *Glen Sannox* and these two, together with MacBrayne's *Columba*, had many exciting races. In 1895 the NBR started a further round of activity with vessels like the 215ft *Red Gauntlet* and in 1906 the Caley at last produced something of an answer to *Glen Sannox* in the shape of the turbine steamer *Duchess of Argyle*. But greater control and co-operation were steadily emerging to produce the pooling arrangement of 1909 and an end to the wilder competition.

The railways continued to operate paddle steamers in the twentieth century but co-operation increasingly replaced competition. In 1909, for example, for the modest sum of 5s 3d (26p) passengers could leave Manchester at 8.55 am, spend $1\frac{1}{4}$ hours on *Philomel* or *Lady Evelyn* on the passage from Fleetwood to Barrow, then go by train to Windermere for a 45 minute sail to Bowness before walking back to Windermere for the return train to Manchester.

The grouping in 1923 increased the scope and desire for rationalisation, while the increasing economic pressures, not only on paddle steamers but on railways themselves, made inevitable a steady decline in the numbers of the former.

CHAPTER TEN

THE ROYAL NAVY

COMMERCIAL life at the dawn of the steam era was beset with difficulties. Not the least of these was the poor service provided by the Post Office. Inefficiency and corruption were commonplace. Indeed, an inquiry of 1787 had revealed that the Secretary to the Post Office was one of the principal owners of packet ships. Matters did improve subsequently although other rackets continued to hinder communications and trade. During the Napoleonic wars, for example, it was not unknown for vessels to be deliberately lost to the enemy for the sake of the insurance money they represented.

However, the Post Office, spurred by growing competition on traditional mail packet routes, was quick to recognise the new development and was among the early users of paddle steamers. The Navy was more complacent and showed every indication of continuing to rely on the traditional 'wooden walls' which had served the country so well for so long. In the early years the only real interest the Admiralty evinced in steam vessels was to cast an acquisitive eye on the Post Office vessels in order to find employment for its officers on half pay and a reserve of trained seamen.

Apart from this interest in the steam packet services, in which the Navy and the commercial interest found a common objective, the former was not really steam conscious and almost missed the paddle era completely. Relying on the greatness of the battles of the eighteenth century and of the men who fought them, the Admiralty was prepared to wait and evaluate any change. On

the other hand it has, in fairness, to be said that the naval authorities did experiment with steam. Although Henry Bell had been rebuffed earlier, Lord Melville did arrange an experiment in conjunction with Brunel in the year of Waterloo. This involved putting an engine into an old surveying schooner but the engine proved much too big and clumsy and the experiment was not a success.

The failure of the first experiment seems to have led to a period of inactivity so far as steam development in the Navy was concerned. Four years with virtually no activity passed before Rennie, at that time 'advising engineer' to the Admiralty, persuaded their Lordships to reconsider the matter. This he appears to have done by hiring the Margate steamer *Eclipse* for a demonstration towing of the *Hastings* which was satisfactorily accomplished against the tide from Woolwich to Gravesend on 14 June 1819. Three years later, eight years after *Majestic* had shown the value of steam for towing sailing vessels and when conveying mails in steamships was no longer a novelty, the Admiralty attitude moderated slightly. In 1822 the Navy acquired the paddle dispatch boat *Comet*. This vessel was 115ft long, 21ft in breadth, and of 9ft draught. She was propelled by two 40hp engines made by Boulton & Watt. She was followed by the acquisition of the dispatch boat-cum-tug *Monkey*, a vessel of 212tons and 80hp which had been launched at Rotherhithe in 1821.

Further paddle tugs followed once the ice had been broken, but the names of these early vessels were not considered worthy of inclusion in the Navy List and the first class-name to appear there is that of the Lightnings of 1827. Indeed, so little did the Navy think of its steam vessels that they were not included among the responsibilities of the Surveyor and consequently their building and design was left entirely to the contractors. There was for some time no proper corps of engineers for the Navy's steam vessels and initially the builders were expected to supply the engine room staff. This attitude of ignoring the paddle steamer was not helped by the other event of 1827, the battle in the Bay of Navarino. There a traditional fleet of British, French, and

Russian vessels mercilessly battered a combined Turkish and Egyptian fleet to leave the distinct impression that all was well on the high seas and that the fleet should be left as it was.

The 1820s thus drew to a close with the Navy possessing a motley collection of paddle vessels and admitting their value only for towage and other ancillary tasks. Neither the vessels nor their crews commanded any real interest or respect either in the high places of the Admiralty or among those who manned the traditional vessels on the high seas. Not only were the vessels varied due to the absence of building specifications, but the men who made up their crews were frequently either inexperienced or not considered suitable for other employment.

The position began to change after Sir James Graham replaced Lord Melville at the Admiralty in 1830. In 1832 the Surveyor to the Navy began to design steamers for conveying dispatches and similar duties and the four-gun *Rhadamanthus* was commissioned. Three sister paddle vessels followed. In the following year the 120ft *Gulnare*, designed by Sir William Symonds, was launched at Deptford. Renamed *Gleaner* in 1837 and lengthened in 1839, this paddler was provided with an armament of three guns.

The next Navy paddle vessel was the 145ft *Tartarus*, built at Pembroke in 1834 and armed with four guns. Two years later the future of the Navy mail steamer became assured when a report by the Commissioners of Revenue recommended an extension of the arrangement which had given the Navy the responsibility for the Falmouth mail packets as early as 1823. Arising from this recommendation, the Admiralty took over the English Channel services from the Post Office in 1837. Ten vessels were taken over including two built at the Chatham Royal Dockyard and the much-travelled *Arrow* which was refitted at Woolwich in the take-over year.

Paddles reached the frigate class in 1837 with the building, again at Pembroke, of Symonds' HMS *Gorgon*. With a length of 178ft and of 1,111 measurement tons, *Gorgon* was fitted with two ten-inch and four thirty-two pounder guns and had a speed of 8·5knots. She was notable as the first steamer with direct-acting, fixed-cylinder paddle engines.

Although the Navy was now building paddle warships it must be acknowledged that there were very material factors weighing against the use of paddle propulsion for ships of the line. Among these factors were the vulnerability of the paddles and the space taken up by the engines. Both were fairly exposed and easy to hit and this would quickly have rendered any paddle vessels *hors de combat*. The position of the paddles and paddle boxes also reduced the number of guns which could be mounted for broadside discharge. With the turret still to be invented this would drastically have affected the whole concept of naval operations which was still based on delivering the heaviest possible broadside. Strangely enough, there was more discussion about the ability of steamers to bear the weight of armament than about any other factor.

Despite the drawbacks of paddle propulsion the Admiralty was to prove almost as slow to adopt the screw as it was to admit the paddle. It was approached in 1836 by the young Swedish engineer John Ericsson. Admiralty officials were towed on the Thames in a barge as part of the practical demonstration but after the trial they reported against the idea commenting that a vessel propelled at the stern would be unsteerable! Ericsson's ideas gained a better reception with the US Navy and eventually found expression in the ten-gun sloop USS *Princeton* which achieved a speed of 13knots with 400hp engines and a six-bladed Ericsson screw.

By the time *Princeton* was launched in 1843 the Admiralty had had second thoughts on the subject of screw propulsion and had arranged for the paddle sloop *Ardent* to be converted, while still under construction, to screw propulsion to the designs of Francis Pettit Smith. On her launching in 1843 the vessel was named *Rattler*. After experimenting with various types of screw it was decided to put to the test some of the points that were being made in the vehement arguments on the respective merits of the screw versus the paddle. Another sloop similar to *Rattler* was selected to take part in these trials. This was HMS *Alecto*, a paddle vessel of 796 measurement tons and with engines of 200nhp.

The first trials were straightforward races and these *Rattler* won easily. Using steam along a course of eighty miles and with a dead calm sea she beat *Alecto* by twenty-three and a half minutes. Next, the two vessels contested a much shorter course in a moderate wind and again *Rattler* won, this time by thirteen minutes. Then came the final race over sixty miles against the wind and the sea and here the screw vessel trounced her list mate by the convincing margin of forty minutes. In a last desperate effort to salvage something from the contest, the supporters of paddle propulsion claimed the better towing power for *Alecto* and to decide this the two sloops were lashed stern to stern for a form of tug-of-war. For a few moments after steam was ordered nothing happened save for an increase in the wash under *Rattler*'s stern and in the spray churned from *Alecto*'s paddles, but then the former slowly gained the ascendancy and dragged her unwilling partner astern at a speed of some 2·5knots.

The experimental *Rattler* was followed by two large screw frigates, *Arrogant* and *Dauntless*. The former had low-power auxiliary engines but the latter was given full steam power. As it turned out, *Dauntless* was not a success because the traditional bluff stern did not give a sufficient flow of water for the screw to grip efficiently. Paddle vessels of the same 850hp proved themselves faster, but the impetus of the French challenge drove British designers on, especially when the screw-driven ship of the line *Napoleon* of 940hp made its debut in 1850. About this period a number of older naval vessels were lengthened and converted to screw propulsion. In 1849 the *Agamemnon* was laid down at Woolwich to become, on her launching in 1852, the first of the Royal Navy's ships specifically built for the screw.

By this time, although still committed to a policy of wooden ships, the Navy had seventeen iron paddle steamers, six of them of the sloop or small frigate variety and including the ill-starred

Birkenhead of 1,400tons. The Admiralty had admitted the existence of iron when it took delivery of the paddle packet *Dover*
which was launched at Birkenhead in 1840. It also acquired
three small iron paddle gunboats in the same year, but for the
time being would not go beyond this. Indeed, in 1842 John
Laird offered in vain to the government an iron paddle frigate
he had built, but the offer was rejected and the vessel was
eventually sold to Mexico.

A few wooden paddle vessels were built for the Navy in the
1840s. From Chatham in 1844 came the 220ft HMS *Retribution*
armed with ten guns and from Deptford in 1845 came the
twenty-gun HMS *Terrible*. *Terrible* was built to the designs of
Mr Oliver Lang and was 226ft long with a beam of 42·5ft and
a depth of 27ft. Of 1,847 measurement tons, she had engines
of 800nhp. In 1849 came HMS *Tiger* from Chatham, a sixteen-
gun, 250ft vessel which surrendered to the Russians in May 1854.
A sister ship *Magicienne* was built in the same year.

The coming of screw propulsion put an end to the prospects
of the paddle in the Royal Navy except for minor duties. A few
special service paddlers continued to be built, largely for work
overseas, but the remaining naval paddle steamers were largely
of the tug variety such as the *Dromedary* which was put to work
in Portsmouth Harbour in 1894. Oddly enough, the special service vessel category included a second HMS *Alecto*, this time a
160ft schooner-rigged, two-funnel paddle steamer built at Poplar in 1882.

Paddle propulsion was, however, to make a comeback in World
War I when, of the 726 minesweepers with which the Navy
ended the war, 52 were hired paddle steamers, 19 were survivors
of the Ascot class of 24 vessels and a further 8 represented the
1918 additions to this class. Designed for shallow-water operation,
the first of these vessels, all named after racecourses, was HMS
Ascot herself. Of 810 displacement tons, *Ascot* was built by
the Ailsa company of Troon although various other shipbuilders
also contributed to the class. She was 245·75ft long and was
propelled by 1,400hp inclined compound engines designed to

produce a speed of 15knots. Her armament consisted of two twelve-pounder guns and she was fitted to carry two seaplanes.

Ascot was commissioned in April 1916 and after being joined by her complement of fifty officers and men she took up her duties in the Firth of Forth until August 1917 when she moved to Grimsby until the following May. A period at Portsmouth followed and *Ascot* then sailed from there on 7 November 1918 destined for Granton. Three days later she was torpedoed and sunk with all hands off the Farne Islands.

Twenty-four of the Ascot vessels were built initially and eight more came into service in 1918. By then, however, the decision had been taken that despite the advantages of draught and manoeuvrability the paddlers were too vulnerable to mines and no more would be built. *Kempton* and *Redcar* were mined off Dover on 24 June 1917, while *Totnes* and *Ludlow* were mined on 29 December 1916 while at anchor off the Shipwash Light Vessel. *Plumpton* was lost at the end of 1918 leaving 27 vessels, including the repaired *Totnes*, to be sold out of the Navy for breaking up. Only two vessels of the whole class were eventually saved from this fate. *Atherstone* was purchased by the New Medway Steam Packet Company and became *Queen of Kent* while *Melton* was later redeemed from the shipbreakers who had acquired the remainder of the class and became *Queen of Thanet*.

The paddle made its strongest impact upon the Royal Navy in the form of paddle tugs. These vessels showed their utility in the very early years by towing men-of-war to and from harbour without the necessity for waiting upon wind and tide and by acting as harbour utility vessels. They survived the challenge of the screw tug thanks to their manoeuvrability in the crowded waters of naval dockyards and establishments and continued at work in appreciable numbers until after World War II.

In the 1950s the Advice class of two-funnelled paddle tugs (not to be confused with the later screw tugs of the Advice class) and some of the Camel class vessels were scrapped. However, four of the latter, *Firm, Swarthy, Sprite*, and *Camel* continued at work at Rosyth, Portsmouth and Devonport. Of typical paddle tug design and with common dimensions (150·75ft long and of 690tons), these vessels had come from various shipyards in the early years of the century. Their turn for disposal came in 1962 which also saw the end of the largest paddle tug ever built for the Admiralty. This was the 178ft, 1,023ton *Pert*, launched by Thornycroft at Woolston in 1916. With compound diagonal engines producing 2,000ihp and 14ft paddle wheels weighing 18·4tons, *Pert* was popularly alleged to be sufficiently powerful to tow three destroyers at one time.

Although *Pert* was the Navy's last steam paddler, the paddle tradition remained alive and in the capable hands of the class of seven diesel-electric paddle tugs designed particularly for towing aircraft carriers with their bow overhang and led by HMS *Director*. Built by Yarrow & Company Ltd of Glasgow *Director*, launched in June 1956, was followed by three vessels from Wm Simons of Renfrew and then three others to make up the class; they were 156·8ft long and of 472·54tons. Most of this class had returned to the home waters of Devonport and Portsmouth by 1969 although *Dexterous* remained at Gibraltar where she helped to handle passenger liners in addition to her naval duties. Almost certainly the last Navy paddlers these squat, powerful, modern-looking vessels make up for the late start in this field by representing one of the most modern presentations of the special attributes of paddle propulsion. The Navy may have started slowly, but it finished well.

CHAPTER ELEVEN

UNUSUAL AND NOTABLE VESSELS

T H E classical form of paddle steamer did not evolve without
several variations appearing, both in the early years of development and later on. Jonathan Hull's 1837 design was for a stern-
wheel vessel and, indeed, in its first form *Comet* was provided
with twin paddles on either side of the hull. One of Patrick
Miller's early designs provided for a vessel with three hulls, but
other designers were not so lavish. The main variations from the
standard design were in search of speed or comfort and took the
form mainly of either double hulls or double paddles.

An early double-hull vessel was the 1817 Mersey ferry PS *Etna*.
She was 63ft long with a paddle wheel between two hulls the
extremities of which were connected by beams to give an overall width of 28ft. Another was *Lord Dundas* which was built in
1831 by Fairburn & Lillie of Manchester for use on the Forth
& Clyde Canal. This vessel was 68ft long and had a beam
measurement of 11·6ft which included a 3·6ft tunnel between
the two hulls. With a draught of 16in and 10hp engines, *Lord
Dundas* was able to carry over 100 passengers between Edinburgh
and Glasgow at a fare of twopence each. About the same time
the stern paddler *Cyclops* was in use on the canal. She had 14nhp
engines giving a speed of 4mph.

The next series of mutations took the form of twin paddles.
In 1838 *Earl of Hardwick* was built with twin paddles driven
by a 20hp engine. A sister vessel *Vernon* showed a clean pair of
heels to two men-of-war in a race in the Channel, but this proved
to be due more to her lines than to her paddles which had a tendency to cause drag. Six years later John Kibble arranged for
Thos. Wingate to build to his designs the Clyde freak *Queen*

116

of Beauty. This vessel, 137·8ft long and of 89·9tons, was engined by Robert Napier. It had fore and aft paddle shafts each side of the hull located between two and three feet above water and each carrying a drum. Between the drums there was a continuous belt with floats attached. *Queen of Beauty* was not a success.

The attraction of lucrative traffic from the 1851 Exhibition led to another search for speed in the shape of the 1850 paddle steamer *Gemini*. Invented by Peter Borrie, this was described as a safety iron twin-hulled vessel of 157·6ft. She cost £14,000 to build and consisted of twin hulls with a single paddle between them, a design which gave a large amount of deck room and carrying capacity for up to one thousand passengers. *Gemini* was a costly failure and made only one sailing when her speed proved only sufficient to stem the tide and certainly much less than the grand hopes she had inspired.

In 1857 came the double-hull steamer *Alliance* which was built by Tod & McGregor with a central paddle wheel. *Alliance* 140ft long, of 30ft beam, 7ft draught, and 51·97tons, worked between Glasgow, Loch Goil, and Arrochar. She was designed by George Mills and had the distinction of being the first Clyde vessel with a saloon on the main deck.

By 1874 comfort had become as important as speed. In this year Thames Ironworks built the twin-hulled *Castalia* of 1,533tons. Each of the two hulls had two funnels and two direct-acting diagonal engines and was fitted with a rudder at each end. Joined by a strong deck with two paddle wheels in tandem between them, the hulls were located 26ft apart to give the vessel an overall width of 60ft, a length of 290ft, and a draught of 14·2ft. The design was intended to reduce sea-sickness on the Dover–Calais crossing and, by means of the duplicate controls fitted, to speed up the turnround in ports. In fact *Castalia* achieved neither objective. She was a bad sailer and her low speed of about 10knots meant that even with a quick turnround she still lost money. Manned by the LC&D Railway, *Castalia* ran as an alternative day boat on the English Channel Steamship Company's day services but was eventually laid up in Granville Dock,

Dover. She was sold in 1884 and became a fever hospital on the Thames.

The 1,886ton *Bessemer* built in 1874 by Earle of Hull was a double-ended vessel with a low freeboard and a saloon pivoted amidships in a further attempt to eliminate sea-sickness. There was a pair of paddle wheels and an engine room at each end of the vessel. On her maiden voyage down from Hull *Bessemer* rode heavy seas quite well but on her trial run to Calais she smashed a paddle wheel. Trouble occurred again on the official maiden voyage when *Bessemer* ran into the pier at Calais and was promptly served with a writ.

The pivoted saloon on *Bessemer* was controlled by an operator using hydraulic rams. He was provided with a spirit level guide and was expected to use the rams to compensate for the motion of the vessel and keep the saloon on an even keel. This proved difficult to do in practice, while *Bessemer* herself was not really manoeuvrable enough to manage the beam winds and cross current encountered at Calais. She was laid up in Granville Dock and then sold for scrap in 1879.

Two years before *Bessemer* was scrapped, Leslies of Hebburn launched what was to be the last word in British double-hulled paddle steamers. This was an 1,820ton vessel based on the same principles as *Castalia* and having a single paddle between two hulls. Called briefly and optimistically *Express*, the new vessel passed into the hands of the LC&D Railway before launching owing to the financial difficulties of the original owners. The deal was ratified after the vessel's sea trials and the steamer was renamed *Calais-Douvres* (I). She was a better seaboat than *Castalia* and attained a speed of 13–14knots which enabled her to complete her maiden crossing in ninety-seven minutes. Even so she was not really fast enough and was sold in 1887 to become a Thames coal hulk.

Apart from paddle steamers notable for their unusual design features there were, of course, many which were notable for their size, beauty, or performance within the framework of the conventional designs. Even when paddle steamers had become commonplace some vessels still managed to stand out from their sister craft because of some distinctive feature or other. Among these was the General Steam Navigation Company's *Trident* which was designed to be the finest steamer in British waters.

Trident was built by Green, Wigram & Green at Blackwall in 1841. Of 971tons gross, she was schooner-rigged with tall topgallant masts, high-standing bowsprit, square overhanging stern, and long sheered bows. She was fitted with engines of 30nhp and, like most vessels of her time, was designed to be armed in the event of war. *Trident*'s launch was a great event but a greater one was to take place in the following year. In 1842 Queen Victoria travelled from London to Edinburgh in her yacht *Royal George* which was overtaken by *Trident* on the voyage north. This led to the latter being chartered for the return voyage, the first time that a British sovereign had made use of a private steam vessel. At the end of the voyage Her Majesty expressed herself well pleased with the whole proceedings. *Trident* remained in service until 1884 and was then converted to a coal hulk.

Perhaps the most striking and forward-looking vessel of all time was the PSS *Great Eastern*. Like the *Great Western* and the six-masted *Great Britain* which proved that iron would float to the many sceptics who doubted this, *Great Eastern* sprang from the genius of Isambard Kingdom Brunel of Great Western Railway fame. At 18,915tons gross register, *Great Eastern* dwarfed its predecessors although *Great Western* at 1,320tons had been a giant of its time and *Great Britain* had been twice this size.

Having conquered the Atlantic and seen the laurels go to Cunard, Brunel turned his thoughts in the opposite direction. Shortly after the halfway mark of the century he placed before the Eastern Steam Navigation Company proposals for a giant steamship to capture the Indian and Australian trade. This was the time of the Australian gold rush and of a Select Committee to establish the best ways of improving communications with India, China, and the Australian sub-continent. Brunel's ideas centred on a ship five or six times larger than any vessel then in use, with superior accommodation and cargo space, a speed of

15knots and a fuel capacity which would eliminate the need to call at intermediate coaling stations.

The work of building the *Great Eastern* was placed in the hands of John Scott Russell & Co of Millwall. The hull was to be on Scott Russell's 'wave-line' principle with 120ft of parallel centre section out of a total length of 692ft. Work started on 1 May 1854 with the laying of a 2ft wide iron bedplate in place of the more conventional keel. The hull was divided by bulkheads and was finally ready for launching on 31 January 1858. Another three months were to pass before a successful sideways launch could be completed and then financial troubles delayed the trials until September 1859.

The *Great Eastern* had five funnels and six masts, the latter designed to carry 6,500sq yd of canvas. In addition to 6,000tons of cargo she was built to carry 800 first-class, 2,000 second-class, and 1,200 third-class passengers and to be crewed by some 400 officers and men. Her 56ft paddles were powered by 1,000nhp engines supplied by Scott Russell and having four oscillating cylinders 74in diameter by 14ft stroke. The four-bladed cast-iron screw propeller was driven by 1,600nhp engines built by James Watt & Co of Birmingham. Using steam at 24–25psi from 10 double-ended tubular boilers heated by 112 furnaces, *Great Eastern* could achieve just over 7knots using her paddle wheels alone and 9knots using her screw.

The first commercial voyage of the *Great Eastern* was made amid much excitement when she sailed from Southampton on 17 June 1860 destined for New York. Further scenes of enthusiasm greeted her arrival there eleven days later. She was not, however, a commercial success due to her relatively low power and speed. Between 1865 and 1873 she worked for the Telegraph Construction & Maintenance Company laying transatlantic cables but after this the great vessel descended to a novelty showpiece and in 1888 was sold for breaking up. A further eleven years was to pass before she was exceeded in size.

An especially notable name in the history of paddle steamers is that of 'Eagle'. Several GSN vessels bore this name which came to be well known to many thousands of pleasure cruise passengers. The company's first *Eagle* dated from 1820 and was only 125ft long and of 56tons. She was followed in 1856 by a 200ft *Eagle* which had been built at Northfleet three years previously. This popular paddler could carry 466 passengers and had a speed of just over 14knots. She carried on her bow the figurehead of an eagle and remained in service for some thirty years.

GSN's third *Eagle* was introduced in 1898 to meet strong competition from the Belle Steamers and New Palace Steamers. With a length of 265ft and of 647tons gross, she was built by Gourlay Brothers of Dundee and had a speed of 18knots. This vessel lasted until 1928 when she was bought by Dutch shipbreakers and her hull became a landing stage on the River Maas. Three more paddle steamers were to bear this fine name before GSN took the title Eagle Steamers into official use in 1932.

It would be an invidious task to try to select and describe all the notable British paddle steamers in this chapter and, indeed, many are mentioned elsewhere in these pages. Apart from the early pioneers and the giants of the ocean routes a few more paddlers do, however, remain worthy of special mention. On the Clyde, probably the most notable paddle steamer of all was Mac-Brayne's *Columba*. Built of steel by Thomson of Clydebank in 1878, *Columba* worked the Royal Route to the West Highlands for fifty-eight years. At 301·4ft she was the longest vessel on the Clyde and from gilded, ornate stem to low, square stern she typified a golden age. All her accommodation and accoutrements justified the £28,000 which she had cost and the steamer remained a firm favourite with the thousands who sailed in her. Indeed she became something of an institution, especially with the local landowners and their guests who used her to get to their homes and shooting lodges beyond Ardrishaig. It was a sad day when *Columba* passed to the scrapyard at Dalmuir in 1936 to become a legend of the Clyde.

An interesting vessel on the Irish Sea was the 400ton *Manx Fairy* built by Laird Bros of Birkenhead. She was described as 'a beautiful little craft, ornamented with blue and gold, with the

H

arms of Man on her paddle boxes'. *Manx Fairy* was purchased for £16,000 to operate between Ramsey and Liverpool. She took up her station at the end of 1853 amid much enthusiasm and to a welcoming verse which ran :

> Oh ! Mona, my darling my heart is still thine,
> My blessing upon thee, I pray;
> And when I am dead, and my spirit is fled,
> Success unto Ramsey, I say.
> The *Fairy* has come, and swiftly has run,
> Her paddles go quickly round;
> Well loaded she is with passengers rare,
> All wishing success to the town.

No sooner had *Manx Fairy* started operating than she was engaged in racing with the Isle of Man Steam Packet Company's *Mona's Queen*, beating her by eight minutes in the first race and then losing the next by ten minutes. *Manx Fairy* was not, however, a complete success for her draught was too great for Douglas harbour and her coal consumption was out of proportion to her cargo space. To make matters worse in August 1857 she ran down and sank the Birkenhead ferry boat *Fanny* which cost her owners £1,775 in damages. The people of Ramsey then bought *Manx Fairy* for £7,000 and kept her at work for four years after which she was sold for £6,000 for work in Sicily.

Three Fairfield paddle steamers deserve a place in this chapter. The first is the 300·4ft *Koh-i-Noor* which was built for the Victoria Steamboat Association in 1892. Costing £50,000, *Koh-i-Noor* was the largest and fastest river steamer of her time and was remarkable in having two rudders, the steam-operated stern rudder being 9ft in length. She achieved 19·5knots on her Clyde trials and then set off for the Thames only to run onto rocks off St David's Head in dense fog on the night of 28 May 1892. She managed to get as far as Milford Haven where she was found to have a draught of 10ft forward and only 4ft aft, only her watertight compartments having saved her from sinking as a result of the 20ft of damage sustained to the bow section. After the damage had been made good, *Koh-i-Noor* started working to Harwich and Clacton in July 1892 and continued until the outbreak of war.

The success of *Koh-i-Noor* led Fairfields to build and own a similar vessel, *Royal Sovereign*, which was launched on 17 April 1893 and was operated by the London & East Coast Express Steamship Service Ltd. The new paddler was 300ft long and of 891 gross tons with a passenger complement of 2,320. She had compound diagonal engines with the two cylinders placed forward of the crankshaft and producing 3,850hp to give a speed of 19·5knots. After a lifetime of working from Swan Pier to Southend and Margate, *Royal Sovereign* was sold to Dutch shipbreakers in February 1930.

La Marguerite came just one year and four days after *Royal Sovereign* and for the first ten years of the former's career on the Thames the two were contemporaries. The 2,205ton *La Marguerite*, 330ft long, was much bigger and more powerful than *Royal Sovereign*. Built by Fairfields for the vsa, later Palace Steamers Ltd, she had compound diagonal engines of 8,441ihp which gave her a speed on trials of 20·82knots. In 1904 she was sold to the Liverpool & North Wales Steamship Company and served it superbly for twenty-one years before making her final voyage on 28 September 1925.

The right to call itself the local paddle steamer with the most varied career might well go to a vessel which was not built until the present century was sixteen years old. In that year W. Hamilton & Company of Glasgow built for the Royal Navy their only contribution to the Ascot class of paddle minesweepers, HMS *Melton*. Like most of her sister vessels *Melton* lay idle after the war until, in November 1927, she was sold to Hughes Bolekow Shipbreaking Company. Then, after suitable conversion and renaming *Queen of Thanet*, the 832ton paddler started working as quietly and competently for the New Medway Steam Packet Company as she had for the Admiralty.

With the outbreak of World War II, *Queen of Thanet* donned her wartime paint, hoisted the Lewis guns onto her sponson mountings and again went to war. Under the command of Captain P. Kitto DSC she worked as an anti-aircraft ship in the Thames Estuary and on the North Sea Patrol before answering the call to Dunkirk. There, amid the bombing and gunfire, she took off many French soldiers. Later in the war *Queen of Thanet* had the risky task of towing lightbuoys so as to delude enemy aircraft into laying their mines away from the main channels. This, like everything else, she did well and when, after the war, she started sailing for the Southampton company as *Solent Queen* her excursions proved very popular. This staunch paddler was eventually scrapped after a serious fire in 1951.

There have, of course, been many other notable paddle vessels but perhaps the final mention in this chapter should be of the veteran *Consul* which had an active life of some seventy years. Built by R. & H. Green Ltd and engined by J. Penn & Sons, *Consul* started her working life in South Devon before the turn of the century. Originally named *Duke of Devonshire*, she typified an era of pleasure paddle steamers and was fitted with a tiny door in the bows to permit her to call at the steeply shelving beaches of Lulworth, Bridport, Seaton, and Sidmouth.

As the minesweeper HMS *Duke*, *Consul*, had an eventful time in World War I including breaking a paddle wheel in a storm in the Middle East. After attending the Dardanelles landings she returned to home waters after the war and passed through several hands until she was acquired by Cosens & Company in 1938. After serving as a contraband examination vessel in the second round of hostilities, *Consul* returned to her old south coast haunts and was then acquired by South Coast & Continental Steamers Ltd. This 257ton, 175ft vessel powered by two-cylinder compound engines spent her last working days in the Weymouth and Portland areas.

CHAPTER TWELVE

PADDLE STEAMER INCIDENTS

DURING the century and a quarter when the paddle steamer was a familiar sight such vessels were inevitably involved in many unusual incidents. These ranged from the amusing to the tragic and from the earliest days to recent years. Some vessels were lucky while others seemed to be unlucky. Some led irreproachable lives, others were involved in adventurous and even illegal activities. The 800ton GSN vessel *Caledonia*, for example, was caught smuggling in 1842. Built at Blackwall in 1836 and fitted with engines of 200nhp, *Caledonia* worked the London to Hamburg run and had something of a reputation for speed. Perhaps this had something to do with her smuggling activities and with her stranding in fog off Flamborough Head in 1864.

Some years were worse than others for mishaps and when, in October 1836, a Greenwich Steam Packet Company vessel ran into *Royal Tar* of Dublin it made the third accident on the Thames in twelve months. In September 1838 there was a notable incident off the north-east coast when the steamer *Forfarshire* was wrecked on the Farne Islands while on a voyage from Hull to Dundee and no less than fifteen people were saved from the wreck by Grace Darling and her father.

The early years were times of much competition and little control. Boiler explosions were frequent, partly because the engineers had to acquire their expertise the hard way and partly because of the demands for steam that racing made upon unsophisticated boilers. One vessel to suffer a boiler explosion on the open seas was *Nimrod*, a steamer of 600tons burden and 300 nhp built by Vernon of Liverpool in 1843. *Nimrod* worked the Cork Steamship Company's Cork to Liverpool route and in a boiler explosion at

Cork in 1856 six people lost their lives. Four years later *Nimrod* broke down at sea and although the *City of Paris* offered a tow the two skippers could not agree on a price and by mutual consent *Nimrod* was left to manage as best she could. Unfortunately this was not well enough and the vessel was wrecked with the loss of thirty-seven lives.

In its early years the P&O suffered a serious setback which nearly ended its career. The vessel involved was *Don Juan* whose first sailing under the mail contract newly secured by the Peninsular Steam Navigation Company almost ended in disaster. The steamer sailed for Cadiz on 1 September 1837 with Arthur Anderson, one of the owners, and his wife on board. After calling at Cadiz and Gibraltar and disposing of the Indian mail *Don Juan* steamed up the coast of Malaga to pick up a cargo of fruit. On 15 September at 2pm *Don Juan* started for home but soon ran into a thick local fog. Hardly had Anderson left the bridge where he had been watching with the captain, Lieutenant Engledue, when the breeze parted the fog to reveal the Tarifa lighthouse in the distance and a group of cruel rocks only forty yards away. There was no time to check the steamer's progress and she struck forward and impaled herself firmly upon these rocks.

After taking stock of the situation, Anderson hired a boat to take him back to Gibraltar with the mails and returned, bringing aid, with the steamer *Medea*. But nothing could be done. *Don Juan* had been lightened by throwing overboard everything movable but still the water gained until only chains held the vessel to the rocks. A considerable amount of specie was taken ashore but was nearly lost to the people of Tarifa who had a long tradition of wrecking and considered *Don Juan* and its cargo to be rightfully theirs. Only the threat of the marines which Anderson had brought along from HMS *Asia* and the promise of a battering from *Medea*'s guns saved the specie—and nearly caused an international incident. *Don Juan* became a total loss and, since she was only partially insured, this was a bitter blow at the outset of the new company's career.

Many incidents occurred as a result of the racing between

rival companies and captains. The English Channel was a notorious racing area and one of the cheekiest exhibitions in any race and of any time took place there. The vessel involved was the 260ton *Ondine* which had been built in 1844 by Miller & Ravenhill for the Dover Royal Mail Steam Packet Company. A condition of purchase had been that she should be capable of outpacing any other cross-Channel vessel and her speed of 12·5knots resulted in a charter by the *Morning Herald* for bringing the Continental news from Boulogne to Dover.

There was considerable rivalry over the carriage of the news and when *Queen of the Belgians*, on charter from the South Eastern & Continental Steam Packet Company to *The Times*, beat *Ondine* by a narrow margin due to the latter's mechanical trouble, revenge had to be sought. *Ondine* challenged the SE&CSP's *Princess Maud* and beat her into Dover by eight minutes. Then, on the return journey to Boulogne, *Ondine* cheekily sailed round her rival twice and still beat her into port. *Princess Maud* later gained a small revenge by achieving a one-minute victory on a run from Dover to Calais. In 1845 *Ondine* was mauled by a storm. She lost her mast after struggling along with a sail and one paddle and eventually had to be towed into Dover by a rescue ship. Two years later she passed to the Admiralty and for some reason became the *Undine*.

One of the peak racing periods on the Clyde was in the years 1860 and 1861. Not only was there intense competition between the railway vessels and the private steamers but the latter also competed with one another. When it is remembered that many of the crews were Highlanders and many of the captains were part-owners receiving a share in the takings, the results can be imagined. The only authority was the River Bailie and his powers were not great so that in their efforts to capture traffic by always being first, steamers not only indulged in some reckless navigation but often skipped piers they should have called at. Until pier signals were introduced in March 1889 under the Clyde Navigation Act of 1887 the fastest boat and the captain with the strongest nerves usually made the first landfall.

At this period the main competition was for the traffic between Glasgow and Rothesay. The main routes were the direct boat service from Glasgow and the journey by train to Greenock and railway steamer from there to Rothesay. Generally the direct boats had the edge but there was little enough in it and for those with good nerves the times were stirring. The three steamers which stood out for speed were *Ruby, Neptune,* and *Rothesay Castle.* Eventually the captain of the former went a little too far and his cavalier treatment of passengers in the interests of speed led to his being removed from his command. *Ruby* often did the journey from Glasgow to Rothesay in as little as two and a half hours.

Among the incidents affecting paddle steamers a number of disasters inevitably appeared. Two particularly bad ones occurred just after the halfway point of the century. The first of these involved the Royal Mail Steam Packet Company which started life with an unparalleled period of bad luck. Among the worst of the events suffered by this company was the loss of the paddle steamer *Amazon*, a 2,851ton vessel built by R. & H. Green and, at the time of her launch, the largest vessel afloat. *Amazon* was 300ft long and had engines of 800hp by Seaward & Capel of Millwall. Built to carry fourteen thirty-two-pounder guns in the event of war, she cost something over £100,000.

There was no hint of the disaster to come when Captain Symons sailed from Southampton on 2 January 1852 with a crew of 110 and some passengers and mails. This was *Amazon*'s maiden voyage and she was bound for Chagres calling only at St Thomas. Not long after sailing a stiff south-west gale was encountered and after battling against this for a while the paddle shafts became hot and the new machinery had to be allowed to cool down. After this had been done everything appeared to be in order, but about midnight of the second day out a fire broke out between the steamchest and the galley on the starboard side.

Before the fire pumps could be got ready the fierce winds had fanned the first flames into a blaze which could not be contained. In a matter of minutes it became clear that the vessel could not survive. The scene was indescribable. The flames had driven the engineers from the engines and the doomed vessel plunged madly on into the storm with the passengers and crew rushing frantically about the fire-enshrouded decks. To make matters worse, the best boats were housed on top of the sponsons and could not be approached because of the heat, while the other boats were mounted on fitments which did not make for easy lowering. The mail boat was swamped and the pinnace hung from a single tackle and flung its occupants into the sea. In the end one of the starboard lifeboats and a dinghy were got away and 59 of the 161 people on board were saved.

The fate of those left on board the *Amazon* must have been terrible. The burning decks gave way beneath some while others plunged overboard in their terror. The whole time the scene was lit only by the fierce light of the flames. Soon after three o'clock the foremast fell overboard to port and the mainmast to starboard, but the mizzen remained standing. By now the fire was raging from stem to stern and the funnels glowed red hot through the flames. The end was not far off and around five o'clock the magazine exploded, the remaining mast gave way and the vessel gave a sudden lurch. Then, to the accompaniment of a great deal of noise as steam and fire met water, the great vessel slid beneath the waves and sank.

The second of these two serious accidents occurred in the same year. At the time, the British forces in South Africa were not doing too well against the Kaffirs and when the *Birkenhead* sailed in February 1852 she had on board 494 officers and men, mostly new Irish recruits, intended to relieve the regiments already fighting the Kaffir chief Makoma. HMS *Birkenhead* was an iron paddle vessel divided into three watertight compartments by iron bulkheads and fitted with engines of 550hp.

Birkenhead arrived at Simon's Bay on 23 February and there exchanged some passengers and took off some horses. She was soon away again and the night was fine and peaceful as the vessel forged ahead at about eight knots. From his position on the paddle box a leadsman was calling out the soundings and there was a comfortable twelve fathoms beneath the hull. Then disaster struck and *Birkenhead* holed herself on a pinnacle of rock. For a moment no one knew what had happened, but then the ship's master-commander ordered the bow anchor to be let go and the quarter and paddle box boats to be lowered.

The accident was then compounded by an order to go astern and as the paddles tugged the huge vessel off the rock so the water rushed into the gap in her hull. To make matters worse the ship was then holed again and the bulkheads badly damaged. While all this was going on the young soldiers had formed up on deck in instant obedience to their officers and showed the utmost calm and bravery. Three boats were got away, mostly filled with women and children, before the ship was holed again and promptly broke in two. The first half sank quickly to be followed by the stern until only the top mast and yard, with a few people clinging to it, was showing above the water. By the greatest constraint there had been no panic which might have swamped the boats that were launched, but now the sea became a mass of struggling humanity most of whom either drowned or fell victim to the marauding sharks. Only twenty-four of the military personnel on board survived thus making this one of the worst disasters in paddle steamer history. *Birkenhead* was believed to have had a large sum in sovereigns on board and several efforts were made to salvage her but nothing of value was ever brought up.

In the issue of 5 September 1878 *The Times* reported 'The wreck of the *Princess Alice* is the most terrible disaster which it has ever been our duty to report!' Built by Caird & Co of Greenock in 1865, *Princess Alice* was 219·33ft long and had started life as the *Kyles* working to Rothesay on behalf of the Wemyss Bay Railway. Her appearance had been considerably altered, and not for the better, when she was acquired by the London Steamboat Company.

On the day of the disaster *Princess Alice* had left Gravesend on a return excursion trip from Sheerness just after 6pm. As she headed back towards North Woolwich pier at a speed of eleven knots, the 800 passengers on board danced to the music of the band or watched the lights come on ashore as the darkness fell.

It was dark by the time *Princess Alice* turned from Barking Reach into Gallions Reach. Her steering lights were lit, her master William Grinstead was on the bridge and the lookouts were at their stations. As usual, traffic on the river was heavy and when the forward lookout sang out 'Vessel ahead' the paddler hugged the south bank a little closer to give the approaching vessel more room. The port-to-port passing regulation applicable on the high seas gave way to local practices in many estuaries and the sighting of the 1,370ton screw vessel *Bywell Castle* gave no cause for alarm at this stage.

On the *Bywell Castle*, proceeding in ballast with the tide, the pilot assumed from the position of the approaching paddle steamer's lights that she was heading across the river to the north bank. He gave the order to turn to starboard to pass astern, but the *Princess Alice* was at the same time swinging to port to pass the larger vessel starboard-to-starboard. By the time those in charge of the two ships realised they had turned on to a collision course the disaster had become inevitable. With all the power of her considerable weight the *Bywell Castle* struck the smaller paddle steamer near the paddle box and drove into her helpless victim for fourteen feet.

The scene on board the *Princess Alice* was one of utter confusion. The throngs of passengers were thrown about by the impact. Few were able to recover themselves before the two vessels drifted apart and the stricken pleasure steamer started to sink. There was no time to launch the boats as the bows and stern jack-knifed and the *Princess Alice* disappeared beneath the waters of the Thames. Six hundred and forty people lost their lives in this tragedy.

It was earlier in 1878 that a paddle tug had played a notable part in bringing the 68·5ft monolith known as Cleopatra's Needle from Alexandria to its present home on the Victoria Embankment. The huge pillar, dating from about 1600 BC was offered to the British Government by the Khedive of Egypt in 1877. Official

funding in such circumstances has always been complicated and
it was left to Professor Erasmus Wilson, a celebrated surgeon, to
find the money and to John Dixon, a civil engineer, to construct
a cylindrical iron 'ship' to convey the obelisk.

The *Cleopatra*, with Captain Henry Carter and a crew of
eight, was launched and taken in tow by the *Olga* in October
1877. On 14 October the cylinder was struck by a heavy sea
and started to roll so badly that her ballast shifted. To avoid a
collision the tow was cast off and *Olga* lost a six-man boat crew
in the dark while trying to take off Captain Carter and his men.
They were, in fact, taken off the following morning and the
errant tow was picked up by the *Fitzmaurice* and taken to Ferrol
in Spain.

To complete the journey the three-funnelled Watkins paddle
tug *Anglia* was dispatched from London. Known as 'Three
Finger Jack', *Anglia* was the largest tug in the Port of London
at the time. She was of 275tons gross and was fitted with 140hp
engines. Using a 15in hawser, *Anglia* arrived in London with
her tow on Monday 21 January 1878 after a six-day voyage
from Ferrol. Cleopatra's Needle was finally erected in September 1878.

Less spectacular but far more numerous have been the many
pleasant incidents associated with paddle steamers ranging from
the memory of a happy voyage to the case of the family who
made several crossings on the Woolwich Free Ferry before realis-
ing that the vessel was not bound for Southend.

Finally, a recent incident involving *Talisman* and *Caledonia*.
The former had just brought her passengers through the Kyles
of Bute to Tighnabruaich, but failed to sail on time on the return
trip. Finally the red-faced crew had to admit that their vessel
had been immobilised by a large jellyfish which had blocked the
water cooling intake. The two consequences of this incident were
that the passengers had to walk a plank over the paddle boxes to
the rescuing *Caledonia* and that the crew of *Talisman* had to
suffer much ribaldry from their colleagues over the next few
days.

CHAPTER THIRTEEN

DESIGN, CONSTRUCTION, AND MACHINERY

T H E paddle steamer pioneers found many problems to overcome in adapting the primitive steam engines of their day to the conventional sailing vessel hull. The early pumping engines were large and heavy and even with a strengthened hull something more compact was needed. With shipbuilding an established trade the main trend, not unnaturally, was to adapt steam engine designs to fit a standard hull, modified only by additional support for the machinery and the provision of external paddle boxes.

Although many ideas were tried, the main course of early marine engine development can be traced back to 1774 when James Watt and Matthew Boulton joined forces to form the firm of Boulton & Watt. Watt's beam engines led directly to the marine side-lever engine which lasted well into the 1860s. In the USA, where *Clermont* owed much to a Boulton & Watt engine, an even more direct development from this firm's pumping engines was the vertical beam engine which emerged about 1822. These engines were reliable, economical, and easy to maintain, but never found favour in Europe.

In Great Britain the earliest union of a steam engine and a ship's hull was when the engine designed for William Symington's steam carriage was mated with one of Patrick Miller's pleasure boats. Symington's specification at the time provided that 'when rotary motions of whatever kind are wanted, two ratchet wheels will be placed upon one or the same axis in such manner that, while the engine turns forward one wheel, the other will be reversed without impeding the motion or diminishing the power so as to be ready to carry on the motion by the time the other wheel begins to be reversed'. The result of applying this was a tiny engine which produced a speed of 5mph despite having cylinders only two inches in diameter. Boulton & Watt would have nothing to do with Symington's original engine but his later version, fitted to the *Charlotte Dundas*, embodied Watt's patent for steam acting on each side of the piston. The piston then worked a connecting rod and crank and the whole arrangement gave birth directly to a generation of marine machinery.

Although Maudslay fitted a powerful side-lever engine to the paddle steamer *Lightning* built at Deptford in 1823, few of the early engines were very powerful, partly due to the inefficient use of steam and partly to the limitations of the early boilers. Restricted in pressures by the constructional materials and techniques available, these internal flue boilers were highly temperamental. Engine failures and boiler explosions were common.

Another problem resulted from the rate of steamer building outstripping the supply of experienced engineers. The engineer of the 1815 *Rothesay Castle* is said to have had no idea of how to reverse his engines, landings being effected by the hair-raising process of cutting off steam and drifting in hopefully! The engineer had noticed that when his vessel was aground overnight the rising tide reversed the engines but might never have realised the significance of this had not James Watt made a voyage in the vessel in 1816.

Boiler explosions were to be a menace for many years. As early as 1817, a House of Commons committee sat to consider the problem. The eventual result was regulations requiring steamboats to be registered. Boilers of passenger vessels were to be of wrought iron or copper, fitted with two safety valves, and tested to three times the working pressure which was not to exceed onesixth of the calculated maximum pressure of the boiler.

The position did improve but boiler explosions remained a risk throughout the 1800s, although during the later competitive periods the cause was more often the temptation to increase pressure by interfering with the safety valves than defects in design or materials. In 1835, while taking part in the Northern Yacht

Club Regatta from Rothesay Bay to Cumbrae and back, *Earl Grey* suffered a boiler explosion which caused the death of six of those on board. As a result of this incident the Clyde Trustees offered a prize of one hundred guineas for any device which would prevent boiler explosions from happening. As late as 1866 the tug *Black Eagle* blew up beneath the Clifton Suspension Bridge at Bristol.

Throughout the 1820s safe pressures were normally between 3 and 5psi with coal consumption as high as 10lb per horse power per hour. The size of the engines and paddles and the space required for coal bunkering limited the size and rôle of the paddle steamer until more compact and efficient machinery brought about improvements in the ratio of paying space to total hull capacity. These factors applied especially to development on the high seas and, coupled with the difficulties of arranging intermediate refuelling, tended to restrict paddles to an ancillary rôle at first. This situation emerges graphically from *Royal William*'s epic voyage to New York in 1833 when contemporary accounts record that the vessel was so overloaded with coal that 'her sponsons were submerged' and passengers were able to lean over the bulwarks 'to wash their hands in the water'.

The 1830s brought many new developments including a breakaway from side-lever engines and flue boilers. David Napier introduced the steeple engine and the haystack boiler which gave a larger grate area and heating surface combined with a lower weight. A steeple engine, so called because it straddled the paddle shaft with the cylinders below and with the crank in a 'steeple' above, was fitted to G. & J. Burns' seagoing paddle steamer *Clyde* in 1832. Four years later the first steeple engine to be fitted to a Clyde river steamer was put into *St Mungo*.

The outline and overall design of the smaller paddle steamer was by now becoming fairly standard with bowsprit, ornamental stern, and conventional rigging maintaining the link with sailing vessels. Funnels were still tall and paddle boxes, while remaining forward of the funnel, were sometimes inset into the hull and linked by a 'bridge'. Change and experiment in this decade tended to affect machinery more than hull design although Napier's finer hull made a growing impact on the 70–100ft length which was normal in the twenties.

Among the other events of the 1830s was the launching by James and William Napier of a long, narrow, and very fast crank boat called *Luna* which had the distinction of carrying the first tubular boiler. In 1838 the 325ton *Columbus* was built to test Howard's 'quicksilver' boiler. After a speed of ten knots on three tons of fuel per day had been achieved and considerable interest aroused, a serious boiler explosion ended this early venture into the realms of higher pressures. In 1839 two notable vessels were built by R. Duncan & Company. *Warrior*, a 128ft wooden steamer of 89·83tons, became the first paddler to be fitted with two funnels placed abeam. *Ayrshire Lass*, engined by Wingate, introduced the geared side-lever engine fed by a square box boiler. About the same time John Gray of Irvine, apprentice of Robert Napier, produced a working model of a compound, surface-condensing engine.

The 1830s also saw the introduction of the first iron paddle steamer on the Clyde. There was considerable opposition to the use of iron for shipbuilding and for a long time many averred that iron ships would not float—despite the fact that iron canal boats are recorded as in use in South Staffordshire as early as 1778. The first iron steamer, the *Vulcan*, was built by Thomas Wilson of Faskine in 1818, but even as late as 1860 the government was against the carriage of mails in iron ships. *Vulcan* was still at work carrying minerals through the Forth & Clyde Canal as late as 1875. In 1821 Charles and Aaron Manby built a small iron vessel which steamed from London to Paris. A second vessel was sent to Paris in sections and put to work on the Seine.

The pioneer iron paddle steamer on the Clyde was the *Fairy Queen* of 39·75tons. Built by John Neilson of Glasgow in 1831, this 97ft vessel was driven by the first oscillating engine on the Firth. She worked between Glasgow and Millport. William Fairburn of Manchester built three small iron steamers in 1831 and later became associated with Lairds of Birkenhead who built

Page 137: (above) Royal Navy diesel-electric paddle tug *Director*; (below) the unusual PS *Castalia* was designed to reduce sea sickness and speed up port turnrounds

Page 138: *(above)* Brunel's giant screw and paddle steamer *Great Eastern*; *(below)* the first PS *Mountaineer* tries to live up to her name in the Sound of Mull

more than a hundred iron vessels before the midway point of the century.

In 1832 MacGregor Laird & Co built *Elburkah* and *Quorra* for an expedition up the Niger and William Laird followed his first vessel, the iron lighter *Wye*, with the iron paddle steamer *Lady Lansdowne* which worked on Lough Derg. Two years later the firm built an iron vessel *Garry Owen* which demonstrated the superiority of iron when, along with some wooden ships, she was driven ashore in a gale. *Garry Owen* suffered considerably less damage than her wooden companions in misfortune. GSN's *Rainbow*, a 407ton iron paddle steamer built at Liverpool by John Laird, was used to experiment with the effect of iron construction on compass deviation.

Iron was used for strengthening ocean-going paddlers but by the time the techniques of iron construction had fully developed the larger vessels were changing to screw propulsion. Iron gave many advantages in shipbuilding. The sides of a hull could be thinner giving a material increase in capacity. Safety was increased as a result of the greater strength of iron and Lloyds recognised this factor by giving underwriting concessions. A further point was the problem of vibration which the use of propellers caused in wooden ships. For such reasons the use of iron increased until by the 1850s most paddlers were being built of iron. The shipbuilders Alexander Stephen & Sons, for example, commenced iron shipbuilding in 1852. About the same time high-pressure steam was coming into use and speeds were reaching the fifteen-knot level.

Direct-acting engines were in use in the 1830s as exemplified by Seaward & Capel's 320hp engine fitted to HMS *Gorgon*, but the main trend continued from side-lever and steeple engines to the oscillating engine. This type was developed for marine use by John Penn & Sons of Greenwich and Maudslay, Sons & Field of London. Out of thirty-four paddle steamers on the Clyde in the 1850s, twenty had steeple engines, seven oscillating engines, while one example each occurred of the diagonal-oscillating, trunk, and rotary types. Twenty of the boilers were of the hay-

I

stack type and five were tubular. All but one of the engines had jet condensers and the boiler pressures averaged 30psi. The big advantage of the oscillating engine was that it took up less space than the side-lever variety. The principle involved mounting the cylinder on trunnions (to allow it to follow the movement of the crank) well below the crankshaft to which the upper end of the piston rod was connected.

From the 1870s steeple engines lost their place first to diagonal engines, then to compound diagonal engines and then to a variety of surface-condensing, tandem compound, and triple-expansion designs. This, of course, only represented the overall trend, for owners and builders had their own preferences and cost was always an important consideration. On the Clyde in the sixties, Thomson built boats with oscillating engines and horizontal boilers, Henderson Colborne & Company's vessels had diagonal engines and haystack boilers, while Tod & MacGregor and Barclay, Curle & Company both went in for steeple engines and haystack boilers. The latter, working at pressures of 40–50psi, were later replaced by 'Scotch' boilers working at pressures of up to 200psi.

Diagonal machinery subsequently gained in popularity and held its position until the end of the century when the engines of the Parson Steam Turbine Company of Wallsend-on-Tyne came on the scene. Compound engines were popular at the end of the century, but although the Swiss were using these to power lake steamers by about 1850, they were slow to catch on in Britain. As late as the 1870s, only Rankin & Blackmore on the Clyde recommended the fitting of compound engines, so many owners being disinclined to pay the higher initial cost. John Elder did more than anyone for the compound engine in this country. He became known as 'the father of the compound engine' and the firm he founded, John Elder & Company, was Fairfield's predecessor.

During the history of paddle steamer development the paddles themselves came in for a great deal of attention. At first floats were fixed and were notable for the mighty thump with which they hit the water and the amount of useless energy expended in lifting water as they emerged. Schemes for improvement were mainly directed towards feathering paddles and altogether over a hundred ideas were patented, although few of them proved practicable. Robertson Buchanan of Glasgow was known to be working on the idea as early as 1813, but the first person to produce a workable scheme was Galloway in 1829. His ideas were taken over by William Morgan of New Cross and in 1830 they were put to the test in trials between the gunboat *Confiance* and her sister ship *Echo*. The result was a 28 per cent increase in speed in smooth water and double this improvement in rough conditions.

The early arrangements for feathering placed the eccentrics between the inner and outer rims of the padddle wheels and necessitated a system of bracing. The position of the eccentric meant that only the inner wheel rim could be attached to the crankshaft, the outer rim being turned by bracing rods connecting the two, while the eccentric was held stationary on a spindle passing through the main shaft. In 1833 Seaward & Capel pioneered the idea of placing the eccentric outside.

There were other schemes for increasing paddle efficiency but these were mainly concerned with alterations to the shape of the floats. John Rennie, for example, fitted diamond-shaped floats to the Thames steamer *Lily* and claimed a 14 per cent increase in speed. Eventually paddle wheels with feathering floats became standard.

The advent of compound and triple-expansion engines had a considerable effect on ship design and operating economics. Coal continued as the main source of power but the new and more efficient engines not only took up less space but derived a greater output from each ton of coal with consequent reductions in bunkering space. The table overleaf illustrates this change.

Passenger accommodation in the early vessels was cramped aft, all the space amidships being taken up by the engines, boilers, and coal bunkers which had to be grouped together to avoid complicated gearing and excessive manual handling of the fuel.

Design problems eased when iron replaced wood for shipbuilding, but the change was dramatic when steel started to oust iron. From this period stems the compact gleaming engine room with engines and auxiliaries taking up less space and permitting a better payload. Steel vessels gave weight improvements of some 50 per cent compared with wood and 15 per cent compared with iron.

Vessel	Engine	Speed Knots	Coal: lb per ihp per hour
Britannia 1840	Side-lever Paddle 740ihp	10	4·7
Scotia 1862	Side-lever Paddle 4,900ihp	14	3·12
Britannic 1874	Compound Paddle 5,500ihp	15·5	1·3
Etruria 1884	Compound Screw 14,500ihp	19	1·9
Compania 1892	Triple-expansion Screw 30,000ihp	22	1·5

The last quarter of the nineteenth century saw not only the introduction of steel vessels and compound and triple-expansion engines, but also the gradual decline of sailing vessels. From over one quarter of a million tons in 1892, the figure of sailing tonnage dropped to 81,882tons two years later and was never again to exceed 50,000tons. In 1892 the average size of steam and sailing vessels was similar at 1,643tons for the former and 1,589tons for the latter, but by 1900 the average size of sailing vessels launched in this country was down to 354tons.

Lairds, who had pioneered iron steamers, were also early in the field with steel vessels. They built a paddler called *Ma Robert* for Livingstone's Zambesi expedition of 1858–64, but she proved under-powered and the water affected her steel plates. Although *Ma Robert* was eventually wrecked on a sandbank, she had helped to usher in the age of steel and with it the final generations of paddle steamers. Hull welding came too late to do much for the paddle steamer. Denny's *King Robert* was welded, but proved so light that she had to be ballasted to give proper paddle immersion.

In the early paddle steamers hulls were of conventional design with a relatively broad beam to support the weight of the paddles and influenced by the general need to make vessels broad enough to support armaments in time of war. Gradually sleeker vessels emerged with fine hulls and raked funnels. *John Penn* of 1859 was a typical example. The typical excursion paddler of the last century had a long, narrow hull with a straight stem and a yacht-like stern. A second funnel and mast was common, but saloons on the main deck were slow to appear. Of forty-three Clyde steamers built in the 1860s, twenty-one had the conventional flush deck, ten had saloons on the main deck and twelve were built with a poop or half saloon aft.

In the 1870s events like the replacement of the old 'knocker' system of signalling by the Chadburn bridge telegraph began to influence design. The conning and berthing function of the paddle boxes remained but in the *Brighton* of 1878 the bridge had virtually become an upper deck. Steam steering gear made its debut in this period, *Iona* (III) on the Clyde being fitted both with this and with the Chadburn equipment in 1873. The traditional helmsman's position aft moved forward of the funnels, but despite the tendency for superstructure to increase in height the conventional raised bridge was slow to emerge and slower still to be located in the forward position.

In the latter part of the paddle steamer era hull design became standard with textbook locations for the paddles in relation to the hull waves and with speed governed by waterline length, trim, and paddle immersion. Stems got flaired a little and sterns rounded, vessels got longer and broader in relation to their length. Upper-deck saloons, single masts, a forward bridge, and shorter funnels became nearly universal. And this is how the paddle steamer will be remembered.

It would be wrong, however, to leave this chapter without some recognition of the deeper effects and the human factors underlying the factual development of the design of the paddle steamer.

In the very early years the problems must have seemed insurmountable. How could a land boiler with its brick flue function in the live, flexing hull of a small vessel in turbulent seas? The answers to this and similar questions cost the early pioneers a great deal of time, anxiety, and money. And those who worked in the early vessels were liable to pay with their lives for the lessons which advanced the design of hull or machinery.

The lot of the crews of the first generation of paddle steamers was no easy one. Until Hall's surface condenser eliminated the problem of de-scaling this would have been no pleasant task during a rough sea in mid-Atlantic. Adjusting the paddle wheel floats ('reefing') to allow for the altered draught as coal and stores were consumed was probably even worse. Imagine too the problems of heavy seas pouring in through the engine room air grates before the modern cowls came into use or of wet coal dust choking the pumps of a foundering steamer.

Yet despite these problems and risks the paddle steamer did develop and at each stage contributed something of beauty. The extensive ornamentation of hulls, saloons, paddle boxes, and even engine rooms rose to quite giddy heights in some vessels and although final forms were more functional, these too produced vessels of grace and beauty.

CHAPTER FOURTEEN

FERRY, TUG, AND OTHER SPECIAL-PURPOSE VESSELS

PADDLE propulsion was not confined to passenger steamers. In addition to its more glamorous rôle in connection with passenger and excursion work, several other types of vessel were developed and contributed to the paddle steamer story. Indeed, the British paddle steamer can be said to have started life as a tug. Jonathan Hull's early design was conceived as a towing vessel, while *Charlotte Dundas* made her name by towing two laden sloops along the Forth & Clyde Canal. Although a number of attempts were made to use paddle tugs on canals these were frustrated by the damage caused by the wash to the canal banks and the main development took place in Britain's harbours and estuaries.

An age-old problem of the sailing vessel was that of making and leaving harbour. Handling such a vessel on the high seas was a very different matter to manoeuvring into a crowded port. There was always the prospect of too much or too little wind and of peculiar local conditions, while ports in the early nineteenth century were frequently inadequate and ill-managed. These factors often led to vessels anchoring in the offshore roads and discharging their cargoes to keels and lighters. This practice meant the extra cost of double transhipment and the potential of paddle vessels for eliminating this was quickly realised.

A paddle steamer specifically built for towage was launched as early as 1814. This vessel, the *Industry*, was used for towing barges from Greenock to Glasgow before the dredging of the channel allowed sea-going vessels to proceed further up the Clyde. Two years later *Majestic* appeared as the first tug on the Thames where, as yet, there were no docks to take shipping off the main channel. With the arrival of powered towage the nightmare of sailing through the hosts of rowboats, hoys and lighters, sloops, and Indiamen began to diminish.

The north-east colliers jumped the paddle stage but the 1814 PS *Tyne Steamboat* took up towing work as the *Perseverance* in 1818 and by 1821 there were fourteen steam tugs on the Tyne. By 'seeking' colliers out to sea and towing them to and from their berths the tugs enabled shipowners vastly to improve turnrounds and towing practice quickly spread to Hull and then to Sunderland and Liverpool. The navy used steam tugs from 1822 and ten years later surplus Tyne tugs started working on the Thames.

Clipper bows, figureheads, and auxiliary sails remained standard for many years, but the initial stubby hull, overshadowed by huge paddle boxes and a tall single funnel were modified as efficiency improved. The earlier vessels often ran short of fuel or failed to manage their tow against a strong tide, but surface condensers, high boiler pressures, and twin engines and boilers brought greater power and often twin funnels.

By the middle of the century hundreds of paddle tugs were at work, making a familiar sight at any port or harbour. Typical of the smaller, wooden variety was another *Perseverance*, South Shields-built in 1849 for the United Steam Towing Company. Of 156tons and with engines of 100nhp, *Perservance* had several owners before she was finally broken up in 1886. At the other end of the scale came the larger tugs built to handle the biggest of ocean-going vessels. Such a tug was the 383ton *Blazer*, an iron paddler built in 1856 by Alexander Stephen & Sons at Kelvinhaugh for the Liverpool Tug Company. Her work included dealing with the American clippers which docked at Liverpool.

With the growth of the holiday and excursion habit in the second half of the nineteenth century tug-owners saw an opportunity to supplement their income by using their vessels for pleasure cruises in the summer months. This development was particularly pronounced in areas like the Bristol Channel where commercial shipping activity and the growing holiday industry were adjacent. As the summer season came along the accoutrements of towing were cleared away and replaced by platforms, seats and awnings in readiness for the happy crowds seeking the benefits of the sea air.

On the East Coast this dual-purpose activity was commonplace. A well-known vessel at Great Yarmouth was PS *United Service* which was built at South Shields in 1871 and came south in the following year. In the summer she carried trippers from the resort's beaches and in winter undertook towing and salvage work as well as towing the lifeboat out to sea. Despite these mixed rôles the summer work was taken very seriously with all the usual amenities provided and a stewardess to take care of the passengers. A well-loved vessel, *United Service* lasted until 1942 when she was struck and sunk by a naval vessel at the mouth of the River Yare. She was refloated, but only to get her to Seago's yard for breaking up.

Another Yarmouth tug which came from South Shields was *King Edward VII* which started work with her East Anglian owners in 1903 and later moved first to South Devon and then to Newcastle. The Great Yarmouth Steam Tug Company also owned *Lord Nelson* which occasionally towed a vessel from the Yarmouth fishing fleet out to sea but spent most of her time on the Yarmouth–Lowestoft run during the day and operating trips around the Yarmouth roads in the evening. *Lord Nelson* had a single mast forward of the black and red funnel and an upper deck stretching from paddle box to paddle box. She and her companion *Lord Roberts* came to do so little towing work that the pair were known as the 'butterfly boats'.

In the South East William Watkins & Co used PS *India* as a dual-purpose vessel from 1891. She proved so successful in the excursion side of the business that Watkins ordered a purpose-built paddler for this work. The result was the 153·4ft *Cynthia* from J. T. Eltringham of South Shields. She started work in the passenger business at Margate in 1893, wintering at the West India Docks and eventually finishing up as a tender at Molville Harbour in Northern Ireland. Her upper works and paddle boxes were white and she had a black funnel with a red band.

From 1860 onwards screw tugs started to appear. At the same time harbours were being improved and the number of large sailing vessels soon began to diminish. Initially the effect of these changes was limited since nowhere did the properties of the paddle wheel show themselves to such advantage as in the tug. Paddle tugs could apply full power quickly in either direction and, by having separate engines for each paddle wheel, could virtually turn on the spot.

For many years both screw and paddle tugs were being constructed. Typical of the latter was the paddle tug *Aid*, built in 1899 by W. Allsup Ltd, Caledonian Works, Preston for service at Ramsgate Harbour. She was 126ft long with a beam of 21ft (35ft across the paddle boxes) and a draught of 6·6ft. *Aid*'s two sets of compound oscillating engines working at 100psi, developed 700ihp and produced a working speed of just over 11knots. The engines were capable of independent operation and the vessel was virtually double-ended having duplicate lights and Napier steam capstans at bow and stern. She was also fitted with Worthington steam fire pumps. Among her tasks, *Aid* included towing smacks and tripper sailing boats, salvage pumping, and accompanying the lifeboat on its frequent calls to the Goodwin Sands.

Gradually the advantages of steam paddle tugs became outweighed as screw tugs improved in design, power, and economy. By the 1920s paddle tugs had retired from the less restricted waterways like the Thames and as diesel propulsion gained ground, paddle tugs retired to the north-eastern ports where coal remained cheap. Back in its native area this type of vessel continued at work at the smaller ports until the early sixties. A decisive year was 1962 when, not only did the Admiralty's last steam paddle tug cease work, but the ranks in the North East were thinned by the withdrawal of *Seaham* and *Elie*.

In 1964 the number of surviving paddle tugs in commercial use dropped to four. At the end of the year the Seaham Harbour Dock Company bought *Eppleton Hall* from France, Fenwick, Tyne & Wear Co for £2,375 and used her as a reserve tug until 1967 when she sailed to the shipbreaking yard of Clayton & Davie

Ltd. The withdrawal for preservation of *John H. Amos* then left *Reliant* as the last steam paddle tug in Britain.

Reliant was built by J. T. Eltringham & Co of South Shields in 1907 for the Manchester Ship Canal Co. Originally known as *Old Trafford*, the vessel passed to the Ridley Steam Tug Company of Newcastle in 1950 and then went to Seaham in 1956 to replace PT *Hardback*. With dimensions of 100ft × 20·16ft × 7ft, of 155·61tons gross and fitted with side-lever engines, *Reliant* typified a generation of British steam paddle tugs and well deserved the last-minute reprieve which saved both her and her Seaham companion *Eppleton Hall* for preservation.

Not only was the North East the spiritual home of the paddle tug and a major building area for such vessels, but it was also the scene of several periods of surplus. One of the effects was the migration from the area of vessels such as the 85ton *Sampson*. She was built at South Shields in 1841, went to Bristol General Steam Navigation and had the distinction of attending *Great Britain* on her trial run.

Another use to which these surplus vessels was put was in the fishing industry. Some paddle trawlers were purpose-built, but several of the displaced north-eastern tugs were put to fishing with long lines and, after proving successful up and down the east coast, were adapted for trawl fishing. Mr William Purdy successfully fitted out the paddle tug *Messenger* for fishing in 1877, while the Reed family had the tug *Ammandale* working from Leith and Newhaven between 1879 and 1881, much to the consternation of the local line fishermen. A paddle vessel, the diminutive *Pyfleet*, was used for dredging oysters on the Essex coast in the early years of this century.

Ferry vessels spend much of their time in manoeuvring alongside piers and across narrow but frequently busy channels, work for which the paddle steamer was well suited. Consequently paddle propulsion expanded quickly in this field, taking over traditional ferry routes and being introduced on new ones. *Elizabeth*, one of the two immediate successors to *Comet* on the Clyde, had a short spell of working the Runcorn ferry about 1814. Two years later *Duke of Wellington* appeared on the Ellesmere Port ferry and *Princess Charlotte* on the ferry to Eastham. The latter also did some towing work and is recorded as acting as a tug for the *Harlequin* in the Mersey estuary in October 1816. About the same time *Etna*, the first purpose-built paddle ferry, began to ply between Liverpool and Tranmere. Her main feature was the provision of the maximum amount of uncluttered deck space.

The other Mersey ferries of the period also operated paddle steamers from an early date. The ancient Birkenhead ferry, once known as the Woodside Royal Mail Ferry, used *Countess of Bridgewater* on charter before putting the purpose-built steamer *Royal Mail* to work in 1822. The same year saw *Seacombe* at work on the Seacombe leg of the Wallasey ferry, inheriting a tradition dating back to 1330 at least. In 1829 *Loch Eck* started to work the Egremont service and in 1834 *Sir John Moore* became the first steamer on the New Brighton run.

From such modest beginnings sprang a paddle ferry tradition of over 150 years. Duties ranged from the modest early local work of the 111ton *Orwell* built at Ipswich in 1826 for the Harwich ferry to services across the busy Thames and short sea runs like that from Portsmouth to the Isle of Wight. Some ferries were privately owned, some publicly, and some by the railways, but all established a reputation for providing reliable, often intensive, services in all kinds of weather and conditions.

The service from Kingswear to Dartmouth exemplifies the less well-known railway ferries. It originated in an Act of 1857 when the Dartmouth and Torbay Railway was incorporated to construct a line to Kingswear and establish a connecting steam ferry to Dartmouth. Operations commenced on 16 August 1864 using the 101ton wooden paddler *Pilot*, a vessel 84·8ft long with engines of 49nhp which had been built at South Shields in 1852. Later in 1864 she was joined by the Blackwall-built iron paddle steamer *Newcomin*, a much longer and narrower vessel of 47tons and with 20nhp engines.

The ancient Neyland-Hobbs Point ferry was taken over from British Conveyances Ltd by Pembrokeshire County Council. An attractive little paddler, PS *Alumchine* worked this service from 1933 to 1956 when unsuccessful attempts were made to preserve her. The 75·8ton *Alumchine* was launched by I. J. Abdela and Mitchell Ltd of Queensferry in 1923. With a length of 80ft and a beam of 17·5ft (31ft over sponsons), her coal-fired 115nhp compound diagonal engines enabled her to carry 220 passengers and 5 vehicles at 9·5knots.

PS *Cleddau Queen* succeeded *Alumchine* on the Hobb's Point ferry service. As originally built by Hancock's Dry Dock Company at Pembroke Dock she was 96ft long and had two two-cylinder compound steam engines which gave her a speed of about 8knots. In her eleventh year *Cleddau Queen* bowed before the winds of change with diesel machinery and screw propulsion replacing her original steam engine and paddles.

The paddle ferry services across the Thames deserve special mention, particularly the Woolwich Free Ferry so well known to all Cockneys. The first steam ferry service in the area was provided by the Eastern Counties Railway when it opened its branch line from Stratford to North Woolwich. The original vessels were the *Essex* and the *Kent*, built at Barking; both 78·5ft long and of 65tons gross. A second railway ferry, that of the Great Eastern Railway from North Greenwich, used the 120ft double-ended vessels *Countess of Latham* and *Countess of Zetland* from Stewart & Latham's yard at Millwall.

From 1880 onwards there was constant public agitation to improve services across the river at Woolwich where the ferries dated back to the twelfth century. The appropriate powers were obtained in an Act of 1885 and services commenced four years later with the paddle vessels *Duncan* and *Gordon* from R. & H. Green of Millwall. Their dimensions were 164ft long, 42ft beam (60ft over sponsons) and 6ft draught. Of 490tons, the vessels were powered by a pair of diagonal, surface-condensing engines for each paddle wheel. The slightly larger *Hutton* was obtained from W. Simons & Co of Renfrew in 1894 and brought the cost of the three vessels up to £45,077.

In December 1922 *Squires*, the first of a new fleet of paddle ferries, arrived to be followed by a new *Gordon* in February 1923. From the yards of J. Samuel White & Co at Cowes, the two vessels cost £69,920. Two further ferries, *John Benn* and *Will Crooks*, were purchased for £74,000 in May 1930. The new vessels were slightly larger than the original ferries and used simple condensing engines. Each ferry had a crew of fifteen comprising captain and mate, four deck hands and deck boy, three engineers, a leading stoker, three stokers and a stoker-cum-storekeeper. In an average day each vessel would carry some 8,000 passengers and 3,000 vehicles and burn anything up to 10tons of coke.

For many years the four paddle ferries were a familiar part of London's river scene. With their disproportionate hulls and tall funnels they were ugly, functional vessels, but they came to endear themselves to thousands who placed their vehicles on the upper deck or travelled in the passenger accommodation below and were conveyed safely across the crowded waterway in every kind of weather. There were incidents, humorous, brave, and sad ones and the war years earned the ferries a special place in the affections of East London. So it was that the advent of the new diesel ferries was greeted in 1963 with pleasure at the improved facilities but with a touch of sadness as the paddlers passed to the breaker's yard.

On the east coast of Scotland road developments ended paddle ferry operation across the Forth and the Tay. Previously nearly 150 years of steamer ferries had seen a grand mixture of vessels, routes, ownership, and types of operation. All this ceased in 1966 with the opening, on 18 August of the Tay road bridge. The last paddle vessel in the area was the Tay ferry *B. L. Nairn*, a 395ton steel paddler built by the Caledon Shipbuilding & Engineering Company Ltd of Dundee in 1929. From 1951 she had worked as relief vessel on the ferry which already had a long history by the time its first steam vessel (the double-hulled steamer *Union* from John Brown of Perth) was introduced in 1821.

The other Tay ferry, the railway link from Tayport to Broughty Ferry, came into being in 1848 and was inaugurated by the Thames-built paddler *Express*. Shortly afterwards, a train ferry service was introduced to obviate the complications of transhipment and a new vessel, the PS *Robert Napier*, was obtained to work the route. She was withdrawn to become the spare vessel for the Forth train ferry route when the Tay bridge was opened in May 1878 but took up her old duties again when the bridge collapsed. This early 'Fifie', as the Tay ferries were known, was finally scrapped shortly after the opening of the new rail bridge in 1887.

The train ferry route across the Forth, from Granton to Burntisland, was also inaugurated with a paddle vessel, the *Leviathan* from Robert Napier & Sons of Govan. Nearly twenty years later, in 1867, the North British Railway acquired the ancient Queensferry passage, but with the opening of the railway bridge the NBR lost its direct interest in ferry operation and utilised contractors to discharge on both routes the obligations in the original Acts of Parliament.

The LNER did work the Queensferry passage again for a time, but in its later years the service was worked by four paddle steamers built, owned, and operated by William Denny & Bros Ltd whose famous pre-war advertisement ran 'How many Channel ships have Denny Dumbarton built?' As the railway bridges across the Firths had brought the decline of the two railway ferries, the Queensferry passage like the Newport–Dundee ferry came to an end with the advent of the new road bridge. And with the Humber Bridge in the offing the days of the paddle ferry are numbered.

CHAPTER FIFTEEN

EXCURSION HEYDAY

PLEASURE sailings have been part of the paddle steamer story throughout its century and a half, but the excursion business reached its zenith in the years immediately before and after the dawn of the twentieth century. These were the years when every resort of any size was served by an excursion steamer, usually a paddle vessel, and when nearly two hundred paddle steamers operated along the south coast alone. This chapter can do no more than describe a few of these vessels and give a brief glimpse of the colourful scenes of the period.

A few steamers spent the whole of their active lives on the same workings, but this was rare and many vessels changed hands several times during the course of their careers. Some had numerous owners and one of these was the 393ton paddle steamer built by J. Scott & Company of Kinghorn in 1899. Named first *Tantallon Castle,* this vessel was intended for the Leith excursion trade of the Galloway Steamer Packet Company. She was a good-looking ship with two funnels forward of the paddle boxes and a full width promenade deck extending from just aft of the mast to the stern.

After only two seasons with her original owners, *Tantallon Castle* was sold to Captain Lee at Brighton and became *Sussex Belle.* When Captain Lee formed his limited company, *Sussex Belle* continued to work the Brighton, Eastbourne, Isle of Wight, Southampton area, but under the ownership of the Sussex Steam Packet Company. With the arrival in the area of the Campbell steamers in 1902, *Sussex Belle* moved north into the ownership of the Colwyn Bay & Liverpool Steamship Company for which she sailed as *Rhos Colwyn.* Next she became *Westonia* on the

Page 155: *(above)* The PS *Star*, a typical paddle tug and general purpose vessel; *(below)* this model of a steeple engine of the late 1830s shows clearly how the name was derived

Page 156: *(above)* The paddle tug *Earl of Dunraven* helping to handle the three-masted wooden barque *Prince Eugene* in the Avon Gorge; *(below)* the Queensferry Passage about 1962

Barry Railway's Red Funnel subsidiary and then, in 1911, when Campbell's took over the Red Funnel steamers, this much-travelled vessel got both a new look and a new name. The new look embraced the loss of the forecastle, while *Westonia* was changed to *Tintern*. After only one season the vessel was then sold to Portugal and became *Alentejo*.

The services provided during this period were as complicated as the careers of the vessels which operated them. All around our shores a variety of paddle steamers provided anything from short evening trips to an inter-pier service and from a jaunt across the bay to a voyage across the Channel. The Belles and the Queens crossed and re-crossed the Thames estuary, while GSN vessels worked to the Continent and up the east coast to Yarmouth. Paddle steamer routes criss-crossed the Clyde and intertwined the islands off the west coast of Scotland, Liverpool was linked with North Wales, and Campbells challenged on the waters of the Bristol Channel and along the crowded south coast.

It was the south coast which provided the most varied of all the selections of steamer services. At Bournemouth, for example, the choice of trip embraced not only Portsmouth, Weymouth, Southampton, and the various piers of the Isle of Wight, but destinations as far afield as Alderney, Cherbourg, and the Torquay area. Each operator had his own agents and made determined efforts to provide a wide variety of choice. Day return fares in the early 1900s varied from three to six shillings (15p to 30p), while Cosens issued fortnightly tickets in books of twelve for fifteen shillings (75p).

Steamer services in this area date back to 1821 when a vessel named *Prince Coburg* started operating two daily journeys between Southampton and Cowes. In 1835 the first excursion operation was introduced when the Portsmouth & Ryde Steam Packet Company's *Lord Yarborough* offered a regular trip round the Isle of Wight.

By the middle of the nineteenth century Cosens and Tizard had several vessels in competition and in 1861 came the massively-titled Southampton, Isle of Wight & South of England

K

Royal Mail Steam Packet Company Ltd. Formed from the Isle of Wight Royal Mail Steam Packet Company and the Isle of Wight Steam Packet Company, the new body operated seven small vessels mostly named after precious stones. In 1865 the firm acquired the Isle of Wight & Portsmouth Improved Steamboat Company Ltd and its two paddle steamers.

With so many increasingly popular resorts along the Sussex and Hampshire coasts there was bound to be a fair measure of competition for the steamer traffic. On the other hand the population of these resorts and their popularity with summer visitors was growing so rapidly that the pressures on the steamer operators were considerably less than those in most other areas. As a consequence there was room both for the large firms and the single-vessel operators and no undue need for them to 'keep up with the Joneses' in the standards and performance of their vessels. This comfortable state of affairs came to an abrupt end just before the new century dawned.

The death of their father, a successful Bristol Channel charter, and increasing competition from railway vessels on the Clyde led Peter and Alexander Campbell to move south to Bristol. Apart from a later tussle with the steamers of the Barry Railway, Campbells had little real opposition and, with their fleet totalling seven steamers by 1897, they decided to try their luck on the south coast where the pickings were more lavish than at the Bristol Channel towns. Accordingly Campbells duly sent *Cambria* and *Glen Rosa* round Land's End to compete with the Southampton company, Cosens, and Bournemouth & South Coast Steam Packets in the Bournemouth and Southampton areas. This was in 1898, the year that the Southampton company acquired *Lorna Doone* only to find that she was no match for the 225ft, 420ton *Cambria* with her big compound diagonal engines. To meet *Cambria*'s challenge the Southampton company obtained the 236ft *Balmoral* from S. McKnight & Company of Ayr in 1900. The new vessel proved capable of matching her rival's twenty knots and some some fine racing ensued.

The popularity of the south coast continued to grow in the new century. Eastbourne, for example, trebled its population between 1881 and 1921. Although Campbells relinquished the Bournemouth–Southampton area and moved east by purchasing the Brighton, Worthing & South Coast Steamboat Company, Bournemouth was still served each season by up to twelve steamers. The east Sussex coast was catered for by R. R. Collard of Newhaven and the Hastings, St Leonards & Eastbourne Steamboat Company Ltd. Including the Joint Railways' fleet and the smaller independent operators like Captain Shippick and his delightful little *Audrey* some forty excursion vessels worked along this coast in the years before World War I.

While all these vessels had their own characteristics and special appeal, they had much in common. Typical, perhaps, of the era was Campbells' *Brighton Queen* which the firm obtained from the Brighton, Worthing & South Coast Steamship Company. This 240·5ft vessel had been built in 1897 by the Clydebank Engineering & Shipping Company and was fitted with two-cylinder compound engines producing a speed of 18·5knots. *Brighton Queen*'s mainmast was removed quite early leaving just the foremast and single funnel. The latter was painted white and the hull black with a distinctive gold lining.

Several south coast steamers were lost during the war but life soon returned to normal after it ended. In 1922 two new companies appeared on the scene, Channel Excursion Steamers Ltd with Belle Steamers' *Woolwich Belle* which it renamed *Queen of the South* and the Cinque Ports Steam Navigation Company with *Emperor of India* chartered from Cosens. Further west the latter were operating *Monarch* and several smaller steamers in the Bournemouth–Swanage area and *Balmoral, Queen,* and *Lorna Doone* in the Solent. Campbells resumed at Brighton in 1923 with *Devonia, Brighton Belle,* and then *Ravenswood,* causing *Queen of the South* to retire to the Thames estuary and Captain Shippick's New Medway Steam Packet Company. In South Devon Cosens' *Alexandra* was vying with the Devon Dock company's two vessels. This firm had only just concluded arrangements to relieve the Cosens competition when Campbells turned up in 1932 with the steamer *Westward Ho*. Despite events like these, life in the thirties was a fairly regular affair and steamer schedules did not vary very much from season to season.

Typical of the paddlers built in this period was the 393ton steel *Gracie Fields* from J. I. Thornycroft & Company of Southampton in 1936. She was owned by the Southampton company and was launched by the 'Lancashire Lass' herself. The dimensions of the new paddler were 195·9ft by 24·9ft beam and 8ft draught. She had two compound diagonal engines with high-pressure cylinders 23in in diameter and low-pressure cylinders of 48in diameter. The stroke was 51in and the engines were rated at 137nhp. Unfortunately *Gracie Fields* had only a short cruising life before she was lost at Dunkirk in 1940.

On the Thames and the east coast the day trip and excursion business took some time to recover from the effects of the *Princess Alice* disaster, but eventually it did so and the years preceding the turn of the century had the flavour of a boom period. Between 1887 and 1889 GSN introduced five new paddle steamers, all of 500tons gross and having a speed of 17knots. Built by J. Scott & Company of Kingston, the five vessels had saloon decks extending the full width of the ship and carried forward of the paddle boxes. Painted in buff instead of the traditional GSN black, the new vessels worked to Yarmouth which was then growing in popularity.

Another notable name on the east coast was that of the Belle Steamers. Known originally as the London, Woolwich & Clacton-on-Sea Steamboat Company and later as the Coast Development Corporation Ltd, Belle Steamers owned seven paddle vessels built by Wm. Denny & Brothers between 1890 and 1900. All had direct-acting, surface condensing engines which produced speeds ranging from the 15knots of *Woolwich Belle* to *London Belle*'s 19knots. The vessels, which were disposed of after World War I, had a single mast and a single buff-coloured funnel with the bridge behind.

The 1890s brought not only an excursion boom on the east coast but also on the Thames. Here GSN was challenged by *Koh-*

i-Noor of the Victoria Steamboat Association, *Royal Sovereign* which was built and owned by Fairfields and operated by the London & East Coast Express Steamship Service Ltd and Palace Steamers Ltd's *La Marguerite*. The vsa was, in fact, introduced with the specific object of breaking gsn's monopoly on the Thames and of getting the Thames Conservancy to improve the piers and place controls on the mooring of barges.

Each morning *Royal Sovereign* loaded her passengers at Swan Pier in readiness for the day's journey to Southend and Margate. Her red funnels with their black tops and two white bands had been lowered for London Bridge the previous night and were not raised again until the journey to Southend was under way. Leaving Southend at 11.50am, *Royal Sovereign* was booked a five-minute turnround at Margate, leaving there at 2.30pm and Southend at 5pm to arrive back at Swan Pier at 8.5pm. In six working days of eleven hours each *Royal Sovereign* would burn 240tons of Best Welsh coal.

Despite these challenges, services from London to Southend, Margate, and Ramsgate were very much the prerogative of the General Steam Navigation Company which for many years offered a daily summer service to all three points with connections off the lt&s Railway. In 1901 'the Magnificent Saloon Steamer' *Eagle* left London Bridge Wharf at 9.10am, calling at Greenwich Pier at 9.30am and Woolwich South Pier at 9.50am before picking up at Tilbury passengers off the 10.15am train from Fenchurch Street. On her return journey *Eagle* left Ramsgate at 3.5pm, Margate at 4pm and Southend at 5.30pm. The return fares were 5s (25p), 4s 6d (22½p), and 3s (15p) respectively and one hundredweight of personal luggage was conveyed free. There was also an 'Express Direct Boat' which left London Bridge Wharf daily at 8.45am for Margate and Ramsgate.

By 1925 the picture had not changed much. From Monday to Thursday *Golden Eagle* left Greenwich at 8.55 am, North Woolwich Pier at 9.25am and Tilbury at 10.40am, getting to Southend at 11.30am, Margate at 1.25pm and Ramsgate at 2.20 pm. There were train connections from Kentish Town and Fenchurch

Street, but the ordinary return fare had risen to 11s (55p). *Eagle* worked this service on Fridays, Saturdays, and Sundays when *Golden Eagle* worked a direct service to the three resorts leaving Old Swan Pier at 9.30 am and returning at 3.5pm.

Another well-known Thames estuary company was the Queen Line of Pleasure Steamers. Dating back to 1837, only three years after the building of Southend pier, the original company was nearly as old as General Steam Navigation. With the advent of Captain Shippick as managing director the Medway Steam Packet Company added the word 'New' to its title and collected together various ex-Belle, ex-Royal Navy, and other paddle steamers to build up between the wars an extensive network of services between the Medway and the Kent and east coast resorts, with regular excursions across the Channel to Dunkirk and Calais. The steamers mostly included 'Queen' in their names with the exception of the 1904 *City of Rochester* which commemorated both an early vessel of that name and the company's home port. This efficient and popular company eventually became part of GSN to form the 'Eagle & Queen Line'.

The excursion tradition on the Clyde started before and lasted even longer than that along the south coast. For many years it was a very extrovert sort of business with the competition engendering high spirits and the readily available liquid refreshments adding thereto. Drunkenness was often a problem and when the Firth of Clyde Steam Packet Company Ltd put the handsome *Ivanhoe* to work in 1880 on the beautiful Helensburgh–Kyles of Bute–Arran route under teetotal conditions many moderate passengers were attracted to the service. All the extremes of the period show up on the Clyde where, the year after *Ivanhoe*'s campaigning owners had to wind up, near riots attended the contest between Clyde Steamers Ltd's paddler *Victoria* and the Dunoon Commissioners over Sunday operation.

The railway steamers on the Clyde did not confine their activities to the regular routes but also participated in the excursion business. The G&SW's *Glen Rosa*, for example, left the yards of J. & G. Thomson Ltd, Clydebank in 1893 to work from

Ardrossan to Arran in the winter months and undertake summer excursions from Ardrossan, Ayr, and Troon. This trim 306ton vessel with single funnel and mast survived until 1939 to become the longest serving G&SW paddler. Her last two years were spent in the Gourock excursion trade after *Duchess of Fife* had replaced her on the Wemyss Bay–Millport run.

An example of the independents was Captain John Williamson's *Queen Empress*, a 210ft paddle steamer of 411tons built at Port Glasgow in 1912 by Murdoch & Murray Ltd. After becoming part of the Williamson-Buchanan Steamers Ltd fleet on her return from war service in the White Sea area, *Queen Empress* worked for ten years running excursions to Ayr, Girvan, Campbeltown, Inveraray, Ailsa Craig, Arran, and 'Round the Lochs'. She was sold to Dutch shipbreakers in 1946 after her second period of war service.

Another well-known cruising paddle steamer on the Clyde was *Lord of the Isles*. The second and best known vessel to bear this name was built in 1891 at D. & W. Henderson & Company's yard in Partick. Of 466 tons and 255·5ft long, she was capable of carrying 1,624 passengers after her promenade deck was extended to the full length of the vessel in 1895. Altogether *Lord of the Isles* had four owners starting with the Glasgow & Inveraray Steamboat Company and finishing with MacBraynes, whose *Iona* and *Columba* she frequently raced through the Kyles of Bute in her early years.

When *King Edward* appeared on the Inveraray route in 1903, the *Lord*'s powerful two-cylinder, oscillating, single-crank engine was frequently called upon for full power as the two vessels raced across Loch Fyne or competed for a berth at Inveraray. Immediately before and after World War I *Lord of the Isles* worked on the round-Bute cruises leaving Glasgow at 10.30am and calling at Govan, Renfrew, Gourock, Dunoon, Rothesay, Port Bannatyne, Tighnabruaich, and Kames. The cost for the full trip in 1921 was 12s (60p) including dinner and tea.

The name Campbell was known in Clyde shipping circles as early as 1836 but when the Campbell paddler *Waverley*, known

as the 'Clipper of the Clyde', came south to Bristol in 1887 and
in 1888 the railway steamers on the Clyde first outnumbered the
private vessels, the family could have had little inkling that it was
leaving one problem area for another. The easy going in the
Bristol Channel which tempted Campbells into south coast operation was rudely shattered in 1905 by the Red Funnel Line
steamers sponsored by the Barry Railway. Another competitor
was William Pockett's Bristol Channel Steam Packet Company
Ltd but the Barry Railway boats were absorbed by Campbells
in 1911 after six years of competition on the water and in
the courts and the BCSPC vessels did not resume after World
War I.

During the period covered by this chapter excursion activity
was commonplace at all British coastal resorts. The main fleets
were, however, not unnaturally concentrated where a number of
resorts or excursion attractions lay not far from one another. The
major area of activity not so far mentioned is that of north-west
England and north Wales. Here the main operator is the Liverpool & North Wales Steamship Company which was formed in
1891 from a Fairfield company and another concern which had
a direct link with the original St George Steam Packet Company.
Operations in this area embrace the coast and sea between Llandudno, Liverpool, Blackpool, Douglas, and Anglesey and at the
height of the excursion era six paddle steamers were at work including *La Marguerite*. Farther north paddle steamers were
operating in the Blackpool area until the early years of the century but then gave way to screw vessels with the notable exception of *Jubilee Queen* which lasted from November 1935 to May
1937 when she was scrapped at Barrow.

The paddle steamer era was a busy, happy, and colourful one,
though not without its excitements. Mishaps were rare even if
steamers did occasionally go aground and although competition
was keen it was more beneficial than harmful. Curious things
happened such as the Barry Railway's attempt to avoid legal
restrictions on ownership by registering its vessels in the name of
private individuals and Campbell's reaction to the Sunday ban

on Clevedon Pier of sailing tantalisingly close but not calling there.

Much effort was put into making the excursions attractive. Music and dancing, book and fruit stalls, and similar facilities were provided, while all the operators paid special attention to catering arrangements. As the Devon Dock, Pier & Steamship Company put it 'passengers may rely upon being supplied with refreshments of the very best quality and every effort will be made for their comfort and accommodation'.

The Devon company carried out its promises and when the *Duchess of Devonshire* operated an excursion to the Naval Review in June 1897 the firm provided lunch for 3s 6d (17½p), tea for 1s 6d (7½p), and supper, after 8.30pm, for 2s 6d (12½p). The latter included cold meats, pigeon and raised pies, and lobster salads with the facility to wash these down with a bottle of champagne for 7s (35p) or a pint of ale for 6d (2½p). All this had to be organised and the size of the supply task can be judged from the fact that GSN in the thirties used 1,500 different kinds of ticket alone.

The variety of steamer tours, often associated with road or rail journeys, was endless. Until 1925, for example, passengers on the *Lord of the Isles* Dunoon to Loch Eck tour were carried to join the loch steamer *Fairy Queen* by a beautiful horse-drawn coach with scarlet-clad postillions. On the other hand, straightforward excursion work was the main activity. This in itself could mean several vessels at a pier at the same time and anything up to 20,000 steamer passengers from one resort on a Bank Holiday. The first vessels were frequently away by 8am and the last to return did so in the darkness.

The special excursions of the earlier years for vegetarians and teetotallers gave way to inter-resort work, trips to see the 'Illuminations' and ventures across the Channel. Whatever form its sailings took, the excursion paddler always gave good value for money and literally millions derived health and pleasure from its activities in this period.

CHAPTER SIXTEEN

PADDLERS AT WAR

QUITE rightly, paddle steamers are associated primarily with excursions and pleasure cruising. They would seem to have little connection with wars and little aptitude for a hostile rôle. Nevertheless, quite apart from the paddle steamers of the Royal Navy, peaceable commercial paddlers have rallied to the call in times of national emergency and have played their part in conflicts all over the world. Paddle steamer participation in warlike activities dates back to Robert Fulton's early warship and to Daniel Brent's armed steamer *Rising Star* of 1820. In the pre-history of the P&O company paddle steamers were chartered out for use in the Spanish War of Succession. The tradition has continued right up to World War II when many commercial paddlers served in a variety of supporting rôles as well as playing a big part in the evacuation of Dunkirk.

In March 1854 Britain and France declared war on Russia and before the conflict ended £15 million was to be spent—or some would say, mis-spent—on hiring vessels for the movement of troops and supplies. Some of these vessels were paddle steamers and some were in the thick of the Crimean activity. One of these was the crack 880ton *Telegraph* which the Belfast Steamship Company had not long acquired from the yards of G. & J. Thomson of Glasgow. To this vessel fell the distinction of bringing home the news of the fall of Sebastopol. Her 685ton sister *Sea Nymph* served in the same sphere. She too made the headlines by living through an exceptionally severe gale in the Black Sea. This gale was so bad that a total of thirty-five vessels foundered and *Sea Nymph* was at first thought to be one of them. This rumour was fortunately unfounded and by superb seamanship her captain was able to bring his ship safely to port. For his skill, Captain Tallin of the *Sea Nymph* was presented by the underwriters with a service of plate.

A large number of British paddle steamers saw service in the American Civil War. In an endeavour to starve the South of the supplies and arms which it needed, Northern vessels imposed a tight blockade of the Confederate ports and although some sailing vessels were able to run the gauntlet they were too few and too vulnerable. At the same time industrial Lancashire still needed its cotton and the emissaries who came to Liverpool to seek fast British paddle steamers to help keep the South supplied with the essentials of war found many British firms willing to act as their agents. It would have been impolitic for these vessels to have been sold openly to the Confederates and many devices were used to conceal their true destination. One of these was to commission or purchase vessels supposedly on behalf of the Emperor of China. The Second China War had just ended and the need for steamers at the Treaty Ports provided ideal cover for acquiring vessels for the Southern States.

Inter-railway competition tended to produce fast vessels and consequently several railway paddle steamers became blockade runners. One which was acquired under the guise of being destined for China was the South Eastern Railway's *Eugenie*. Of 428tons and built by Samuelson of Hull in 1862, she later returned to her native shores to become *Hilda* of the GSN fleet and work between London, Margate, and Ramsgate.

Typical of the steamers to become blockade runners was *Douglas* (I) of the Isle of Man Steam Packet Company. Launched in 1858 and the first of the company's straight-stemmed steamers, *Douglas* (I) was a fast vessel and produced a record run of four hours and twenty minutes from Liverpool to Douglas. Through the agency of a Liverpool firm she was sold to the Confederates in 1862, painted in a service coat of grey and given a new name. Only one year later the vessel's career came to a sudden end while on a journey from Charleston to Nassau with a cargo of cotton. As she neared the Bahamas she was chased by the Federal steam gunboat *Rhode Island* which fired salvo after salvo and chased the fleeing Confederate ship into the three-mile limit. There was little difference between the speed of the two vessels and as the blockade runner fled in the channel between the reef and the land her pursuer kept up the pressure until she holed her quarry's boilers and caused her to be run onto the beach.

Another Thomson vessel, the *Giraffe*, was sold to the Confederates the year after the Douglas (I) and for the sum of £30,000. *Giraffe* had worked G. & J. Burns' Clyde to Belfast service and then made several profitable trips for her new owners before she fell to the gunboat *James Adger*. At the time she was carrying a load of arms and army clothing under the name of *Robert E. Lee*.

The agents for the Confederates were always on the look-out for fast steamers which would be able to outrun the Federal gunboats. The 230ft *Venus* was built by C. J. Mare & Co of Millwall as a China mail packet but when she produced a speed of 17½knots during her trials she was transferred to the Confederate cause where she was regarded as the finest ship of the whole fleet. In 1863 the Northern forces reported that *Venus* was working regularly between Bermuda and the Southern ports and that they had been quite unable to stop her. A few months later, in the October of that year, the blockade runner's luck ran out. She was sighted by the *USS Nausemond* and at first managed to outstrip her pursuer. Then *Venus* found herself cornered among shoals where she was eventually destroyed.

As the conflict lengthened and goods became scarcer the demand for vessels to run the blockade increased. In answer to this demand Alexander Stephen & Sons built two blockade runners in the record time of six weeks. These were iron paddle steamers 210ft long and 552tons gross and their construction represented no mean shipbuilding feat. Not unnaturally several of the purpose-built vessels were laid down in Liverpool. Among these were the first steel paddle steamer to cross the Atlantic and the notorious *Colonel Lamb*. Built in 1863 by Jones, Quiggin & Company, 296ft long and of 1,132tons, *Colonel Lamb* proved highly successful in her adventurous career and was one of the blockade runners to return to commercial service after the war. However, she eventually blew up in the Mersey, a fitting end to a colourful vessel.

At the outbreak of the 1914–18 war the Admiralty requisitioned many paddle steamers for the work of laying and sweeping mines, flotilla and squadron supply, carrying ammunition and stores, and acting as fleet messengers and troop transports. The Clyde made a major contribution as did the south coast fleets and companies like GSN and the Isle of Man Steam Packet Company. Not only were the ships taken but the crews went with them and the senior staff of the operating companies were enrolled to serve on such bodies as route committees, shipbuilding committees, and the National Martime Board which dealt with the manning of ships in Government service.

General Steam Navigation lost three of its paddle steamers during the war. One of these was *Philomel*, one of the finest ships in the company's fleet. Under the command of Captain H. J. Wilson she was at the head of a convoy between Brest and Bordeaux on 16 September 1918 when she was torpedoed and sunk. The officers and crew managed to get the boats away before *Philomel* went down and were duly picked up by the USN patrol vessel *Rambler*. *Golden Eagle* was another paddle steamer of the GSN fleet which went to war. For most of her service she plied as a troop transport between France and Southern England and altogether carried over half a million troops. Later in the war she was converted to a seaplane carrier.

At the outbreak of war the Isle of Man Steam Packet Company had a fleet of fifteen steamers of which eleven 'joined up'. Five were paddle steamers. Of these one, *Empress Queen*, sank while engaged in troop carrying, one returned to peacetime service after the war and three were purchased by the Admiralty for net-laying and anti-submarine work. Of the latter three, *Mona's Isle* (III) had the most varied career. Intended primarily as a net-laying vessel, she also had a period patrolling the west coast of Ireland in readiness for the expected attempt to land arms there. On another occasion she assisted in salving guns from the torpedoed *Arethusa* and she was also the base ship for the rescue of £86,000 from the wreck of a Dutch steamer which had been torpedoed outside the Cork lightship.

Empress Queen was the largest and swiftest paddle steamer of her day but she came to grief and was wrecked during fog on 1 February 1916. The steamer foundered on Bembridge Ledge, Isle of Wight and although she had 1,300 soldiers on board at the time all were rescued. The wreck remained visible above water for another three years. The company's supreme heroine was *Mona's Queen* which accounted for an enemy submarine in February 1917. While on a voyage from Southampton to Havre the paddler spotted the submarine lying on the surface a short distance away. Although a torpedo was hurriedly fired at the advancing steamer she held her course and the missile passed harmlessly across her bows. The next minute the submarine was caught in the *Queen*'s port paddle wheel and sustained such damage that she flooded and sank almost immediately. For this gallant action Captain William Cain and his crew received generous monetary tributes from the Admiralty and from private sources. The crew would, at this time, have been a standard one laid down by the Admiralty consisting of the captain, a chief officer and a second officer, chief, second, and third engineers, donkeymen, firemen and trimmers, deckhands, a steward, and a mess-room boy.

A Clyde veteran called upon to serve in the 1914–18 war was the venerable *Duchess of Rothesay*. Built by J. & G. Thomson at Clydebank in 1895, this 234ft steamer had been the pride of the Caledonian Steam Packet Company fleet at the height of the rivalry with the G&SW steamers. *Duchess of Rothesay,* whose great rival was *Jupiter,* took over the Gourock–Arran run from the teetotal *Ivanhoe* and soon made a name for herself. For her minesweeping service in the war a high wheelhouse was erected in front of the rakish single funnel and gun platforms constructed fore and aft. With a sweep attachment inclined outwards from her stern she presented a gaunt contrast with her peacetime rôle in 'Caley' colours and crowded with holidaymakers. In addition to sweeping over 500 mines *Duchess of Rothesay* achieved the unusual by towing a disabled German Zeppelin into harbour at Margate. After this it came as an anti-climax when she sank at Marklands Wharf during a post-war refit in 1920, a sea cock having been carelessly left open. After four weeks the veteran was raised to resume her peacetime sailings until 1939.

Eagle (III) was altered in a similar way to *Duchess of Rothesay* except that the bridge structure had to be built aft of the funnel and extending each side of it. After serving as a minesweeper *Eagle* (III) was refitted for her peacetime workings from Glasgow to Rothesay and Lochgoilhead, her bridge being moved forward of the funnel and a small upper deck being added. In World War II, *Eagle* (III) visited Dunkirk and thus maintained a fighting tradition which extended back as far as the first *Eagle* of 1851 which had been a blockade runner in the American Civil War.

Marmion was lost to a mine in World War II after surviving the previous conflict in which she served as a minesweeper attached to the Dover patrol. Between the two wars *Marmion* was laid up from 1921 until 1927, but then worked regularly between Rothesay and Craigendoran. When she was being converted to a minesweeper, *Marmion*'s promenade deck was extended to the bows. Similar treatment was accorded to the 536ton *Waverley*, the first excursion steamer built for the North British Steam Packet Company, which had been launched from the yard of A. & J. Inglis on 29 May 1899. The extension was perpetuated in the post-war refit when the bridge was brought forward of the funnel before *Waverley* took up regular service on the Craigendoran, Arrochar, and Lochgoilhead run.

Built in 1912, the 210ft, 411ton *Queen Empress* typified the best of designs in Clyde paddlers of the period. She was plated right forward and the bridge was placed in front of the single funnel. *Queen Empress* worked as a troopship between Southampton and France during the first war and while so engaged she collided with a destroyer off the French coast. Luckily the Clyde paddle steamer *Duchess of Argyll* was in the vicinity and was able to take the crippled *Queen Empress* and her cargo of one thousand troops in tow. After a period as a minesweeper based on the Tyne, *Queen Empress* sailed to the White Sea and took part in active service there as an ambulance transport. After World War II this grand Williamson-Buchanan vessel was sold to the Dutch for breaking up.

The Belle steamers, some of which also went to the White Sea, survived the war without loss despite the varied incidents in which they became involved. Based as minesweepers, first at Swansea and then at Harwich, their duties included sweeping in front of naval vessels and this took them as far afield as the French and Danish coasts. In 1919 *Walton Belle* and *London Belle* had no sooner got rid of their minesweeping gear than they were re-engaged by the Admiralty and fitted out as hospital tenders. In the May of that year they were sent via the North Cape to the White Sea and spent four months around Archangel ferrying wounded men from the Russian campaign to homeward-bound ships.

The White Sea was not the only foreign theatre in which British paddle steamers found themselves far from home. They were used as hospital vessels by the Inland Water Transport Division in Mesopotamia. Four vessels were specially built for this work and each was designed to cater for 98 British and 96 Indian patients. These paddle steamers were 218ft long. They were fitted with water-tube boilers supplying compound, surface-condensing engines which burned seven tons of coal each twenty-four hours to give a speed of 8knots.

World War I saw an end to five paddle steamers from the south coast fleets. Campbell's *Brighton Queen* was mined off the Belgian coast in October 1915 and three other paddle steamers were sunk while sweeping mines. These were the Joint Railway's *Duchess of Richmond*, the Southampton company's *Stirling Castle* and Cosens' *Majestic*. *Stirling Castle* went down off Malta in 1916 while *Majestic* was swamped off Oran as a result of listing and water coming in through an open port. The unluckiest vessel of all was the Southampton company's *Princess Mary*

Page 173: (above) Fairfield's 1,554ton *La Marguerite* owned by Palace Steamers and then by the Liverpool & North Wales Steam Ship Company; (below) the second MacBrayne steamer to carry the name *Pioneer*

Page 174: (above) A blockade runner of the American Civil War, the Liverpool paddle steamer *Colonel Lamb*; (below) a typical paddle steamer on the Thames, 1904

which survived the war but foundered after the Armistice due to passing over a wreck in the Dardanelles.

Although their ranks had been slowly thinning year by year, Britain's paddle steamers again rallied round as World War II started. The GSN vessels were very soon at work and during the first three days of September 1939 the decks of eight steamers were thronged with hosts of bewildered and excited children carried from Gravesend, Dagenham, and Tilbury to the relative safety of Felixstowe, Lowestoft, and Great Yarmouth. Altogether 19,578 children were safely carried to the reception areas, over half of them embarking from the Ford Motor Company's jetty at Dagenham on Friday 1 September. *Golden Eagle* alone carried over three thousand youngsters as her first task in a varied wartime career. On her bridge at the time was Captain J. A. Traynier who served with the Royal Navy in Scotland and the US Navy in Iceland before being reunited with *Golden Eagle* at the end of the war, this time under the aegis of the RAF and maintaining the balloon barrage in the River Scheldt at Antwerp.

Along with many other shipping companies the GSN sent the best of its peacetime pleasure steamer fleet to the beaches of Dunkirk. Eight vessels took part in the epic and each had its own special experiences, but here again the rôle of the notable *Golden Eagle* is worth describing. On her first trip she picked up and brought back survivors of the *Waverley* who had been machine-gunned in the water after their ship had been bombed and sunk. The next time *Golden Eagle* went back she lay offshore all day under bombing attack and artillery bombardment while her boats ferried troops from the shore. On her third and final trip over this grand vessel was one of the last to leave the scarred east pier and left behind her only a destroyer and the block ships.

One of the Woolwich Ferry paddlers, *John Benn*, tried to get to Dunkirk but she was not cut out for speed and after running into mechanical difficulties had to turn back. But the ferries were to have their hour of glory on the night of 7 September 1940 when the might of the Luftwaffe was directed at London's docks and East End. So intense was the bombing that the north bank

L

of the river soon became an inferno and part of the Silvertown community was cut off. Then the ferries came into their own and by the light of the blazing fires and through patches of burning oil carried the beleaguered citizens to the comparative safety of the south shore.

The south coast fleets and the Clyde were naturally well represented during the hostilities. *Talisman* became the anti-aircraft vessel HMS *Aristocrat* while *Jeanie Deans* took up the same duties after her recovery from a bombing attack in 1941. Not all the Clyde steamers survived the war. The handsome, two-funnel *Juno* which had worked the Gourock–Rothesay run from June 1937 was sunk by bombing, while the 1934 paddler *Mercury* was lost on Christmas Eve 1940 after striking a mine. Another casualty was the 1897 veteran *Kylemore* which was sunk by a German bomber on 21 August 1940 while engaged in net laying at the mouth of the Wash. *Kylemore* had served in the south as *Britannia* and with the G&SW as *Vulcan* before being sold to Captain John Williamson to work from Glasgow to Rothesay until 1935 when she passed to the LMS railway.

Of the Bristol Channel and south coast paddle steamers which participated in the Dunkirk evacuation, four did not return. Among these was the *Devonia* which, after being beached, was later salvaged and towed away to Germany. Two Southern Railway vessels became mine victims in 1941, while *Her Majesty* succumbed to an air raid on Southampton. The response of the paddle steamer to the war needs of the country had been handsome but there were some sad gaps in the post-war pattern of refit and return to cruising.

CHAPTER SEVENTEEN

THE TWENTIETH CENTURY

T H E paddle steamer owed much to the fact that the only power unit available in the early years of steam was the slow-speed reciprocating engine which was ideal for use with large paddle wheels revolving at a relatively low speed. The development of screw propulsion and improvements in marine engine design did not dramatically affect the position while coal remained cheap and stokers were easy to come by. As these factors changed and turbine and diesel machinery gained ascendancy so the paddle steamer waned. After the turn of the century its main sphere was esturial work and in the excursion trade, leaving the short sea routes to modern screw vessels. On the LNWR's Holyhead–Greenore route for example, two screw vessels were introduced in 1895 and the last paddle steamer was withdrawn in 1902.

Passenger services on the Thames experienced very mixed fortunes in the last twenty-five years of the nineteenth century. As a London County Council pamphlet of 1905 put it, 'the *Princess Alice* disaster was a deadly blow to all the pleasure services'. The excursion trade fared better than the regular steamboat operations which became spasmodic and poorly patronised until, in 1901, the River Thames Steamboat Company announced its intention to discontinue such services.

Considerable pressure for the restoration of a service was then put on the London County Council by politicians, the press, and by public opinion generally. After studying the matter carefully and encountering a number of setbacks the LCC obtained the necessary powers in 1904. Orders were hurriedly placed for twenty-three steamers at a cost of £195,000 and the service was inaugurated by the Prince of Wales, later King George V, on

17 June 1905. Operating at fifteen-minute intervals, the service ran between Greenwich and Hammersmith calling at twenty-three piers en route. The steamers took forty-five minutes for the journey from Greenwich to Westminster and although fares were charged in [old] penny stages it was possible to travel the complete distance for fivepence single and eightpence return. Unfortunately this brave venture did not succeed. The first winter was foggy and the second summer wet. In addition the steamers proved difficult to handle in the tidal conditions of the Thames, partly because of their over-powerful engines. There were mishaps and accidents and the paddlers went aground more often than they should. Although nearly five million passengers were carried in 1906 the service still lost over £40,000, with the total losses, including capital losses on the boats and piers, soon mounting to nearly ten times this sum. As a result the Thames Steamboat Service became a leading point of contention in the election of 1907, the Municipal Reform party making capital of the fact that the losses meant asking people to pay higher municipal rates. With their return to power the Municipal Reformers gave the service a further short trial from May to October 1907 and then closed it down in conformity with their election pledge. The service ended, the boats were disposed of and the piers destroyed.

Over a lengthy period the redundant paddle steamers were dispersed to a variety of places. Fourteen were sold for a new Thames service while others went to excursion operators. Three went to Swiss concerns. One of these, the *Ben Johnson*, was purchased for £500 and sailed up the Rhine to Basle where she was moved by rail to Lucerne for re-assembly and a second maiden voyage in March 1911 as the *Rhein*. This typical vessel was of some 120tons and, with diagonal compound engines, could carry 530 passengers at 12·5knots.

On the west coast of Scotland, not only had there been a boom period in the last decade of the nineteenth century, but the second generation of paddle steamers had fallen due for replacement and many well-known paddlers had been built in this period. Most of these lasted until well after World War I and some even survived the second conflict. Among the latter was the gallant *Lucy Ashton*. Built at the Seath yard at Rutherglen in 1888 for the North British Steam Packet Company, this 224ton vessel lasted until February 1949. Even then she was to have a further short period of useful life.

She was stripped at Denny's yard of her superstructure and paddles and fitted with four jet engines. In this form she was used on the Gareloch measured mile to evaluate various forms of hull resistance without screws or paddles disturbing the water.

Other paddle steamers lasted until the 1920s and 1930s but, although the present century dawned with plenty of paddles at work on the Clyde, a significant event occurred in 1901 when Denny of Dumbarton built the world's first passenger vessel to be propelled by turbine machinery and *King Edward* started sailing from Broomielaw on behalf of the Turbine Steamer Syndicate, later Turbine Steamers Ltd. The geographical considerations in the area and the beauty of the scenery have meant a continuing steamer tradition, but the introduction of *King Edward* struck the first real blow at the paddle steamers' erstwhile supremacy. The manoeuvrability of paddle vessels continued to be a considerable asset, but with a top speed of 20·5knots *King Edward* was faster than most paddle steamers of the day and could even produce a knot or so more than the very fast *Glen Sannox*.

More turbine vessels were introduced in the first decade of the century and the paddle steamer cause was not advanced by the abolition of competition under the railway companies' working agreements of 1906, nor by the rationalisation which followed the grouping of the railways which became effective in 1923. By 1910 steamers were beginning to be laid up and the older vessels used only on special or relief duties. Some events seemed to stay the process of erosion, like the introduction of DEPV *Talisman* and the further round of paddle steamer building in the mid-thirties, but slowly the process went on, hastened by the war and the slump and temporarily retarded by the boom years.

Among the notable vessels built in the 1930s for the Clyde area was the 427ton *Marchioness of Lorne* delivered by the Fairfield

Shipbuilding & Engineering Co Ltd to the Caledonian Steam Packet fleet in 1935. *Marchioness of Lorne* was a single-funnel vessel with concealed paddle boxes and no upper deck. Her triple-expansion diagonal machinery was designed for economy rather than speed and she could make only 12knots. During World War II she was the only LMS paddler left on the Clyde and worked in drab grey colours until she was refitted in 1946 for the final nine years of her career. *Jupiter* from the same yard relieved the *Marchioness* on the Holy Loch service from February 1946.

On Loch Lomond, where steamer services dated back to 1817, paddle vessels had natural advantages which kept them immune from the challenges being experienced on the Clyde. In addition the picturesque setting in which the steamers operated helped to stave off the decline in demand which was beginning to become apparent elsewhere. The two North British Steam Packet Company vessels introduced just before the turn of the century were followed by the 304ton *Prince Edward* in 1912 and then by two ex-LCC vessels. The latter were *Earl Goodwin* and *Shakespeare*, renamed *Queen Mary* and *Princess Patricia* respectively.

Despite the gradual increase in screw vessels and the general rationalisation which affected all steamer services, paddle steamers remained the mainstay of the excursion business for many years. In addition several companies undertook longer journeys where the outward and homeward trip could not be accomplished in one day. Period returns were generally offered on all the regular services so that those going on holiday could, if they wished, start off with a steamer journey to their destination.

In 1904 GSN were operating a steamer service from London Bridge Wharf (8.30am), Greenwich Pier (8.50am), South Woolwich Pier (9.10am), and Tilbury (10.15am) to Yarmouth. This service, which operated each summer on Tuesdays, Thursdays, and Saturdays between 25 June and 14 July and daily thereafter, had a return working from Yarmouth at 8am. Return fares were 8s 6d (42½p) saloon and 6s 6d (32½p) foredeck with children under twelve conveyed at half price. Perambulators and bicycles cost 1s (5p) each, while dogs were charged 2s 6d (12½p) for the single journey.

There was a surplus of shipping after the 1914–18 war. The replacement of war-time losses was done on an over-optimistic basis and by 1922 ten million tons of shipping was laid up throughout the world. Two and a quarter million tons of this was under the British flag with 30,000 officers and men unemployed. This situation and the economic difficulties of the late twenties did not stop firms like GSN from continuing in the excursion business, but all operators were obliged to think carefully before introducing new vessels and deciding upon the design to adopt.

GSN had tried the triple-screw *Kingfisher* on the Thames, but her lack of manoeuvrability at the piers and the excessive wash created by her high speed of 21knots had influenced the company in its decision to acquire *Golden Eagle* in 1909. This vessel had the distinction of being the first Thames pleasure steamer to have triple-expansion engines. The lack of success achieved by the New Medway Steam Packet Company with the twin-screw, ex-Gravesend–Tilbury ferry vessel *Gertrude* influenced GSN in its introduction of *Crested Eagle* from J. Samuel White & Co in 1925. Among the innovations brought by this 1,110ton vessel were oil-fired engines giving a speed of 18·5knots and a first-class saloon forward on the main deck. She was fitted with a bow rudder and with telescopic funnel and hinged mast to allow passage under London Bridge. On her return voyage she would be turned at Greenwich and use the bow rudder to complete the journey stern first so as to be ready for the following day's sailing. Until 1931 *Crested Eagle* operated to the Kent resorts and then went to work the new summer service to Clacton and Felixstowe.

In 1932 Cammell Laird & Company built the last GSN paddle steamer—apart from those acquired with the New Medway company in 1936. With four decks, twin masts, and a single funnel, the company's 116th paddler was a beautiful vessel, worthy to uphold a proud name and a long tradition. Before deciding on steam and paddles for *Royal Eagle*, the company had examined the alternatives very thoroughly, but modest draught, manoeuvrability, and high deck capacity were still sufficient to sway the decision. In this connection comparison with the principal dimensions of the 1949 twin-screw vessel *Queen of the Channel* is revealing :

	Gross Tonnage	Length (feet)	Speed (knots)	Passenger Capacity
Royal Eagle	1,539	292	18	1,966
Queen of the Channel	1,500	271·9	18·75	1,500

In the Bristol Channel P. & A. Campbell Ltd gradually fought off the challenges of the steamers based on the Welsh coast until, with the acquisition of *Lady Moyra* and *Lady Evelyn* from W. H. Tucker & Co Ltd of Cardiff, the White Funnels finally triumphed over those of red and yellow. The acquisition of these vessels and a new steel paddler, the 553ton *Glen Gower*, enabled Campbells to resume their Brighton activities in the following season, 1923. Nine years later Campbells started working from Torquay and Plymouth, serving the resorts from Bournemouth to Penzance. The use of *Westward Ho* on this work forced the Devon Dock, Pier & Steamship Company out of excursion work. They sold their two vessels and although a new company ran *Duchess of Devonshire* in 1933 and 1934 this grand vessel was lost at Sidmouth in August 1934 when she dragged her stern anchor and was washed broadside onto the beach.

The position elsewhere on the south coast is dealt with more fully in another chapter but brief mention should be made of the general position in the South West. Here the effect of cheap coach excursions was felt in the years between the wars but many paddle steamers were at work in the earlier years of the century. In 1912, no less than fifteen steamers were at work in the South Devon estuaries. The Kingsbridge–Salcombe service which had first used a paddle steamer in 1857 again had a paddler in 1906 when the 53ton *Ilton Castle* was put into regular service on the route. A twin Willoughby steel paddler *Kenwith Castle* was introduced in 1914 and continued until the two craft were sold in 1927 to the GWR whose omnibus services had undermined their trade.

The present River Dart Steamboat Company Ltd took over four 'Castle' steamers from its predecessor in 1906. In 1923 and 1924 the company acquired its last paddle steamers, the 91ton *Totnes Castle* and the 94ton *Kingswear Castle*. The former was sold in 1963 along with the 1914 *Compton Castle*. At the mouth of the Dart estuary, the last paddler on the lower Dartmouth–Kingswear ferry, the 61ton iron *Dolphin* built by Harveys at Hayle in 1869, was scrapped in 1908.

The Saltash, Three Towns and District Steamboat Company marked the new century with the addition to its fleet of a 62ton steel paddler, *Prince Edward*, in July 1904. In April 1910, when the fleet consisted of three screw and six paddle vessels, the firm sold out to the Plymouth Pier and Pavilion Company Ltd which continued the ferry services and pleasure trips to the Yealm, round the Sound and up the Tamar until the slump of the mid-1920s. Another operator in this area, John Parson of Millbrook, took delivery of the 64ton *Britannia* in 1900 and the 99ton *Hibernia* in 1904, both from Philips of Dartmouth. This operator also acquired one of the ex-LCC vessels, the 126ton *Brunel* for which he paid £500 in 1909, two years after the fleet was first put up for sale.

The Plymouth estuaries typified one of the paddle steamer scenes of the pre-war years. Emerging from a main activity of carrying produce to the Plymouth markets into a predominance of excursion cruises, the various small paddle steamers also engaged in a variety of other activities including ferry and towing work. Despite their size the vessels and their crews had engaged in some determined rivalry at the turn of the century and competition remained keen for a number of years. The excursions were cheap and popular and with the opportunity to cruise, dance, and listen to a band for an afternoon for less than two shillings both individual passengers and the organisers of outings were regular patrons of the Calstock and other trips.

At the other end of the scale companies like GSN, MacBraynes, Campbells, and Belle Steamers typified the way the excursion and coastal business could become a highly organised activity.

The Coast Development Corporation, for example, had by 1905 opened piers at Southend, Felixstowe, and Lowestoft and its seven Belle Steamers operated an intricate pattern of services based on vessels sailing from London to Yarmouth and along the Kent Coast, from Yarmouth to London and from the Orwell southwards. By interlinking these operations a considerable variety of regular and special trips was available during the week, while on Saturdays the services were adjusted to cater for the Londoners going to or coming from their holidays at the Kent and Essex resorts.

Now that we have briefly looked at the paddle steamer in the twentieth century in some of the main and some of the minor areas of operation, it is appropriate to pause and consider what conditions were like on board. The continuing need to attract passengers ensured a high standard of comfort, cleanliness, and catering although vessels on local excursion work were also worked with an eye to accommodating the maximum number of people. For the crews the hours were long and the rewards modest. On the Manx steamers for example, a seaman's wage was 28s (£1·40) per week for sailing all hours. Only if the vessel did a double trip, to Liverpool and back for example, was anything extra paid and then this was only an additional 2s (10p). The girls in the refreshment room and the cashiers got 12s 6d (62½p) per week and their keep, while the stewardesses were paid 10s (50p) for which they were expected to keep the cabins tidy and take care of their lady passengers. The sailors had their own forecastle accommodation but the girls slept in the ladies' cabins when the vessel was in port. They kept their bedclothes stowed in lockers under the settees and took their meals in the dining room.

Life was hard and the hours long but everyone was happy. Often when the vessel lay at anchor the crew would organise a sing-song. If the weather was fine there might even be a dance up on the main deck. And the crew were not above having a bit of fun at the expense of the passengers. On one trip to Fleetwood a steamer hove to for some hours with engine trouble. In response to a question about the delay from an old lady the chief engineer was heard to blame matters on 'the chief engineer taking his tea'.

While the period from the beginning of the century to the outbreak of war brought only a natural development of the factors working against paddle steamers this process changed and quickened between the two wars. The losses of World War I were not fully replaced and the years of economic crisis took their toll, particularly in the less dense holiday areas. At Scarborough, for example, the Scarborough Harbour Commissioners had operated the paddle steamer *Kate* from 1866, the *Alexandria* from 1879, and the *Cambria* from 1899. However, the ranks of the paddlers which sailed up and down this coast between Whitby and Bridlington then started to thin. PS *Scarborough*, for example, withdrew in 1914, while the Crosthwaite Steamship Company's *Bilsdale* ceased operating in 1934.

Like many other activities, paddle steamer operation suffered in the difficult years of the late twenties and early thirties. Even as economic conditions improved so the motor bus and the diesel engine flourished and the railways tasted the first fruits of rationalisation. Consequently decisions as to a further generation of paddle steamers required much heart-searching. In fact, the newly-formed Southern Railway started its replacements as early as 1924 when *Shanklin* took over from *Duchess of Richmond* on the Portsmouth sailings.

The new vessels of the thirties included further SR paddle steamers with the 684ton *Sandown* displacing *Duchess of Kent*. For two years the latter worked between Ipswich and Clacton as the New Medway Steam Packet Company's *Clacton Queen* before passing to the Mersey & Blackpool Steamboat Company and being renamed *Jubilee Queen*. Then came the 566ton *Ryde* in 1937. Built by Denny Bros, *Ryde* represented something of a new era and was the first of the Portsmouth fleet to have triple-expansion machinery. On the Clyde the same builders produced the 623ton *Caledonia*. Just as the trend since 1900 had been to place the funnels forward of the paddle boxes following grouping of the boilers, so with the new vessels of the thirties the trend was towards concealed paddle boxes, simulated windows, and an altogether more functional outline.

And so British paddle steamers in the twentieth century approached the second great conflict. Their ranks were thinner than in 1914 and the reduced number of operators had a large proportion of modern vessels. Even so the holiday crowds of 1938 and 1939, still enjoying the cruising tradition of previous generations, could continue to find a few veterans at work to add variety to their excursions.

CHAPTER EIGHTEEN

DECLINE AND PRESERVATION

T H E years which followed World War II brought with them
the swansong of the British paddle steamer. The war and its after-
math played some part in this, while rising costs and changing
tastes added to the pressures on the operators, particularly of
pleasure steamers. However, although the peace celebrations were
destined to be followed by the lean years of economic recovery,
some new paddle steamers were ordered and grey veterans of the
war were given an extensive refit as part of the preparations for
a relaxation from the rigours of conflict to the peaceful pleasures
of coastal cruising.

In addition to the vessels lost during the war, some of the
paddlers which did return were unfit for further service and were
scrapped. The Southampton company's *Balmoral* and *Lorna
Doone* and Campbell's *Cambria* and *Westward Ho* came into
this category. Replacements included not only two of the ex-
Ascot class of minesweepers from the New Medway company
but, significantly, a new *Balmoral* in the shape of a twin-screw
motor vessel from Thornycrofts.

In the Bristol Channel, P. & A. Campbell Ltd of Cardiff started
their post-war operations with a break from the traditions of over
fifty years. Until delivery was taken of the screw vessel *Empress
Queen* as an early replacement for its war losses, Campbell's
White Funnel fleet had consisted exclusively of paddle steamers.
The firm later reverted to tradition by ordering a new paddle
steamer from Charles Hill & Sons Ltd of Bristol in 1945.
Launched in the following year, *Bristol Queen* proved a distinctive vessel 245ft long and with a displacement of 961tons. With

twin funnels and masts, a cruiser stern and concealed paddle boxes she was soon a favourite in the White Funnel fleet. Her triple-expansion, oil-fired engines were supplied by Rankin & Blackmore Ltd of Greenock.

Campbells took delivery of a second new paddle steamer in 1947, the 238·5ft *Cardiff Queen*. Of 765 gross tons, this handsome vessel was built and engined by the Fairfield Shipbuilding & Engineering Company Ltd of Glasgow. Her three-crank, triple-expansion diagonal engines produced 2,200ihp and gave *Cardiff Queen* a speed of 17·52knots during her trials. Prior to her disposal she shared the White Funnel workings between the main coastal towns from Mumbles to Ilfracombe and the excursions to Lundy, the Cornish resorts, and the Scillies.

Another post-war paddle steamer was the 693ton *Waverley* built in 1947 by A. & J. Inglis Ltd of Glasgow. The 240ft long *Waverley* has oil-fired triple-expansion engines which produce a speed of 17knots. This twin-funnel vessel has a passenger complement of 1,350 and succeeded the North British Railway vessel of the same name built in 1899.

Maid of the Loch was also built by A. & J. Inglis, in 1953. At 191ft she is the longest vessel on Britain's inland waters and, with her twin funnels and rakish mast, the *Maid* is an extremely attractive vessel, her white hull finding an admirable setting among the hills and heather which surround Loch Lomond. She has oil-fired steam compound engines which give a speed of 14knots and was transported by road in sections and erected at Balloch, the pier from which she now commences her summer services.

In many ways 1953 was a significant year. With the exception of vessels like *Queen Empress, Lucy Ashton,* and others involved in the post-war settling-down period, the main phase of retirements started in 1953 when the new Clyde diesel vessels were introduced. This resulted in the withdrawal of vessels such as the *Marchioness of Lorne* and the *Duchess of Fife,* while *Prince Edward* was broken up on her native Loch Lomond in 1955.

With the nation's improving prosperity public tastes had changed. New and more sophisticated entertainment and the growth in continental holidays drew people away from the traditional pleasures of coastal cruising. With the relative costs of paddle steamer operation also rising the result was a fresh round of withdrawals in the 1960s. Vessels like the Caledonian Steam Packet Company's *Jupiter* passed from the scene to be followed by the four Woolwich Free Ferry paddlers. Next *Whippingham* was withdrawn from the Portsmouth–Ryde service and was eventually sold to Belgian shipbreakers.

After the 1963 summer season the ranks of the remaining paddle steamers were reduced by the withdrawal of Kent's *Medway Queen* and Devon's *Totnes Castle*. The latter eventually sank in Bigbury Bay while under tow to shipbreakers at Plymouth. When *Sandown* retired, British Railways was left with only one paddle steamer on the south coast. This suffered even further when *Consul* ceased to ply her trade and lay forlornly at anchor in the Dart estuary under her original name of *Duke of Devonshire*. For twelve months she awaited a buyer but the requisite £9,750 was not forthcoming. Eventually *Duke of Devonshire* was consigned to the breakers and arrived at Southampton in October 1968 after spending some time weatherbound in Poole Harbour while on tow from the River Dart.

In the north DEPV *Talisman* was withdrawn in 1966 and was broken up in the following year by Arnott Young & Company at Dalmuir. The ex-LNER vessel built by Inglis in 1935 had been laid up in 1953, but re-appeared in 1954 with new British Polar engines. Hoped at one time to breathe new life into the paddle steamer cause, the gallant *Talisman* seemed to have shrunk into shabbiness in her closing years. *B. L. Nairn* and *Cardiff Queen* were also withdrawn in 1966. Some interest was shown in the following year in taking the latter to the Clyde and then, at the beginning of 1968, she was purchased by a Chepstow firm with the intention of using her as a night club or discotheque at moorings on the Wye or Usk. Despite the example of *Compton Castle*, now leading a gay and well cared for retirement as a showboat and cafe at Kingsbridge, this proposal came to nothing.

The year 1967 started badly for the paddle steamer enthusiast. The scene at Weymouth Harbour at the beginning of the year must have been a sad one with *Princess Elizabeth* laid up not far from the berth where *Embassy* awaited the arrival of the German tug *Fairplay* to tow her to a shipbreaking grave at Antwerp. The 371ton *Princess Elizabeth* had been built in 1927 at the Southampton shipyard of Day, Summers & Company and had worked to and from the Isle of Wight until 1959. After her war service she had re-appeared with oil-fired engines and resplendent with many brass and copper fittings. Frequently filmed and televised, there were plans to convert her to a floating hotel, but this came to nothing and in October 1967 she was towed back to her birthplace to be broken up on the River Itchen by the same firm who were breaking up the historic Princess flying boats. A last minute reprieve came at the beginning of 1968 when the vessel was purchased with the idea of using her as the centrepiece of a south coast marina. At the end of the following year planning permission was refused and *Princess Elizabeth* was sold to a Mr Hickman for £3,000 for use as a London restaurant and conference centre with a Dunkirk bar and museum.

With the decline in the number of paddle steamers came a growing awareness among devotees that the time was approaching when this type of vessel would be extinct. At the same time railway preservation interests were achieving some notable successes. From these two influences came the formation of the Paddle Steamer Preservation Society which, as it slowly increased in size, began to study seriously the possibility of acquiring a paddle steamer in order to preserve the type. Initial thoughts in this direction centred around PS *Alumchine* which, at the time of her displacement from her ferry work in Pembrokeshire, was the smallest paddle steamer in the British Isles. However, the attempt was premature and the society had to let the diminutive vessel pass for scrap in 1962.

Next on the list for attempted preservation was the 316ton

Page 191: *(above)* The 624ton PS *Jupiter*, introduced in 1937, took over the Holy Loch service in 1946; *(below)* from the same builders came the post-war paddler *Cardiff Queen* for P. & A. Campbell Ltd

Page 192: *(above)* After retiring from ferry work PS *Alumchine* became the first paddle steamer preservation candidate; *(below)* Ferry vessel PS *Tattershall Castle* leaving Hull for New Holland, 1967

Medway Queen which had been built by the Ailsa Shipbuilding Company of Troon in 1924. Owned by the Medway Steam Packet Company Ltd, a subsidiary of GSN, she was the first of the Queen Line of steamers and the first Medway steamer to have the top deck carried forward to the bows. Her normal post-war run had been from Chatham to Southend, back up the Medway and over to Southend again in the middle of the afternoon. This the Eagle and Queen Line Handbook 'Seawards' described as a 'service which is operated by the smart paddle steamer *Medway Queen* with regularity and a marked degree of popularity'. A worthy candidate for preservation, known and loved on the wartime strands of Dunkirk and the peacetime beaches of the south-eastern resorts, *Medway Queen* made her last service voyage from Strood Pier to Southend and back on 8 September 1963. She was dressed overall for the occasion and ceremonial farewells took place at each port of call. Even *The Times* recorded the event.

The preservation society found an ally in Fortes, the London catering firm. The aim was to moor *Medway Queen* in the Thames and use her as a floating restaurant with a section reserved for a museum of Dunkirk and of the steamship era. Fortes acquired the paddler but then ran into difficulties in finding a suitable mooring and it looked as if *Medway Queen* would follow her contemporaries to a ship-breaker's yard. Terms for sale to a Belgian firm had actually been concluded when a last-minute reprieve brought the vessel into the hands of A. H. & C. B. Ridett who gave her a new lease of life as a nautical centre and club in the Medina river on the Isle of Wight.

One of the consequences of the proposals put to the Scottish Transport Users Consultative Committee by the Caledonian Steam Packet Company for re-shaping its steamer services on the Clyde was that PS *Jeanie Deans* became spare and was put up for sale. A grand vessel of 839tons, *Jeanie Deans* had been built by Fairfields in 1931 for the LNER and had returned to the Clyde in 1945 for a post-war refit. In September 1965 there were reports that she had been purchased by the Paddle Steamer Pre-

M

servation Society but, in fact, the vessel came south to the Thames as *Queen of the South* operated by the Coastal Steam Packet Company Ltd.

In June 1967 *Queen of the South* started her new season with a marathon celebration that got no farther than the Pool because of an engine breakdown. Then, fresh from overhaul and fitted with a new bow rudder, the vessel started working from Tower Pier and Greenwich Pier to Southend and Herne Bay on Mondays, Tuesdays, and Wednesdays and to Southend only on Thursdays, Saturdays, and Sundays. On these days an evening cruise was operated at 8.45pm. The bad luck which had prevented sailings in 1966 showed itself again in the form of boiler troubles at the beginning of the season and again on 25 July when the vessel had to be withdrawn. Subsequently the owners went into liquidation and the vessel was 'arrested' by the Admiralty Marshal as a consequence of claims for unpaid mooring fees. After a court hearing in October 1967 *Queen of the South* was sold to a firm of Belgian shipbreakers and this gallant attempt to maintain the paddle steamer tradition on the Thames came to an end as the fine vessel was moved from her moorings at Erith to her grave at Antwerp.

Success finally came to the preservation society when PS *Kingswear Castle* came to the end of her service with the River Dart Steamboat Company. This river paddler was 94tons gross, 108ft long, and 28ft over paddle boxes and was built by Philips of Dartmouth in 1924. Her steam reciprocating engines were built by Cox & Company about 1880 having been fitted to *Kingswear Castle* from an earlier Dart steamer. The price of £600 was a special one for sentimental reasons and this was raised by members of the society.

With *Kingswear Castle* chartered to Ridetts for care, maintenance, and operation and with society working parties already contributing to this end, the Paddle Steamer Preservation Society ended its tenth year in 1969 with much achieved. The same year saw the formation of the Pleasure Steamer Historical Trust aimed at preserving and exhibiting any material relating to British pleasure steamers. The Trust, co-operating with the PSPS, took over responsibility for the material staged in the Pleasure Steamer Era room at the Maritime Museum for East Anglia at Great Yarmouth.

Returning to 1967, a 'Grand Long Day Cruise' (six and a quarter hours from Cardiff to Tenby via Weston and the Gower Coast) in September heralded the swansong of *Bristol Queen* after only eleven years service. The year 1968 dawned with a proposal to use *Bristol Queen* as a maritime museum for Bristol. This idea came to nothing but at least no further passenger vessels were taken out of service and, indeed, the year was an active one for the few paddle steamers which remained.

This year was also notable for an extension of the preservation interest beyond the passenger steamer field. During the year the Dorman Long Museum purchased the paddle tug *John H. Amos* on behalf of the Teesside Borough Council and restoration work was commenced at Middlesbrough Dock in 1969. This 202ton vessel, built by Bow McLachlan & Company Ltd, Paisley in 1931, had worked locally for the Tees Conservancy Commission carrying workers to the dredging fleet.

In 1969 two other north-east paddle tugs were rescued from the scrapyard. In June *Reliant* sailed from Seaham Harbour to Grays as part of the National Maritime Museum's plan to preserve and exhibit the greater part of the vessel. Her sister vessel, *Eppleton Hall*, had already been sent for scrapping but was saved just in time by the San Francisco Maritime Museum.

Fifty-four years old when she left Britain, *Eppleton Hall* was an ideal candidate for preservation. Everything, from varnished woodwork and golden scrollwork to the oil lighting, typified an era. The undertaking was, however, no light one for though her redemption cost only £2,500, the bill for renovating the vessel and making her safe to cross the Atlantic came to over £60,000.

The three Scottish paddle steamers had a busy 1968 season. By Easter *Waverley* and *Caledonia* were at work from Craigendoran, the latter undertaking cruises for the Clyde River Steamer Club and Rutherglen West Parish Church and participating in the annual Millport illuminations. Despite continued publicity, *Maid of the Loch* made a loss in 1967 but her patronage was growing year by year and the three vessels were back at work again in 1969. Then, as the decade ended, came the sad decision to dispose of *Caledonia*.

On the Humber, Associated Humber Lines continued to operate the three paddle steamers working BR's Hull–New Holland ferry despite rumours of a Humber Bridge and threats from hovercraft services. Confirmation of the bridge proposal in mid-1969 seemed likely to save the vessels from replacement and ensure that for several years passengers would still have the opportunity of seeing a stoker at work feeding the ferries' coal-fired, triple-expansion, three-cylinder engines.

The two earlier vessels, *Tattershall Castle* and *Wingfield Castle* —both 210ft long and of 556tons—were built in 1934 by Wm. Gray & Company of West Hartlepool to replace earlier and much less attractive vessels. With single funnels abaft the paddle boxes, they were the first paddlers built by the firm for some years. *Lincoln Castle*, an Inglis vessel, is similar to her sisters although the funnel, buff with a red band and black top, is forward of the paddles. She was launched in 1940, but owing to compass trouble on her wartime journey round the north of Scotland did not take up her ferry duties until the middle of 1941.

The three vessels, which perpetuate a ferry tradition dating back to AD 100, operate all the year round carrying passengers, vehicles, and some parcels traffic. The erstwhile summer river cruises were dropped through lack of support but *Lincoln Castle* undertook both charter and television work in 1968 and 1969.

On the south coast PS *Ryde* undertook charter work in 1968 and 1969 as well as her regular ferry task between Ryde and Clarence and South Parade Piers at Portsmouth. Among her special voyages was an excursion in connection with the return of Sir Alec Rose after his famous voyage round the world. In addition to providing a venue for a reunion of those who served in her during the war and undertaking a PSPS charter to Southampton Docks, *Ryde* included a cruise as an Edwardian floating gin palace as part of an advertising promotion on the Thames. Add to these examples the visit of the Derby Opera Company to the Humber ferries to help them with their production of 'Showboat' and it becomes clear that the traditional variety of paddler work has not diminished.

A few other paddle vessels remained at work as the decade drew to a close. In addition to *Ryde* and the Navy paddle tugs at Portsmouth and Gosport two paddle ferries plied in the south. Working between Lymington and Yarmouth (IoW) was the BR car ferry *Farringford*. This 489ton vessel built in 1947 and capable of carrying 796 passengers and 40 cars has diesel-electric propulsion. The upper ferry on the River Dart is also a diesel-electric vessel. Built in 1960 by Philip & Sons, the vessel is captive and is guided by chains in place of a rudder. The 1970s started with *Ryde* being offered for sale thus thinning the paddler ranks even further.

Some paddle vessels still existed on the inland waterways in 1969. In fact, it is on the canals—where the paddle was largely rejected—that the happy ending for this book can be found. In 1960 a retired naval engineer, Lt-Commander Wray-Bliss converted an old narrow-boat into a passenger carrying vessel at Bath. Fitted with paddles because of the amount of weed in the Kennet & Avon Canal, the well-named *Charlotte Dundas* carried an increasing number of passengers from 1962 when she entered service.

By 1969 the *Charlotte Dundas* was working in the Pewsey area under the auspices of the Kennet & Avon Trust and her place had been taken on the Bath–Bathampton excursion work by a further, purpose-built paddler, the *Jane Austen*. These two vessels may well mark not only the beginning and end of the conventional paddle steamer era but also, with the efforts of the other preservation interests, herald a final chapter which will ensure that the contribution made by our paddle steamers and the men who manned them to our national wellbeing will not be forgotten.

SUPPLEMENTARY NOTES

As indicated in the introduction to this book the technical data included have been strictly limited in order not to obscure the main theme. It may be, however, that some additional data would be helpful to those with special interests and accordingly supplementary notes on various aspects of the main text have been included below.

CHAPTER ONE   THE BIRTH OF THE STEAMBOAT   (Up to 1820)

Page 21   The original dimensions of the *Comet* are also recorded as 43·5ft long by 11·33ft beam by 5·65ft draught.

CHAPTER TWO   THE PADDLE STEAMER DEVELOPS   (To c 1825)

Page 30   In August 1813 a small paddle steamer, the *Telegraph*, had her final trials on Breydon Water before going into regular service between Yarmouth and Norwich. Her regular schedule involved a departure from Turner's bowling green, Yarmouth at 7am with the return from Foundry Bridge, Norwich at 3pm. The vessel blew up at Easter in 1817 killing 22 people and injuring others.

Page 30   Early paddle steamers of General Steam Navigation :
1824—*Eagle, City of Edinburgh, Belfast, Eclipse, Venus, Brocklebank, Earl of Liverpool, James Watt, Lord Melville, Royal Sovereign, Soho, City of London, Hylton Jolliffe, Victory, Hero*
1825—*Camilla, Attwood, Prince Frederick, Superb, Talbot*
1826—*Duke of York, Magnet, Columbine, George IV, Harlequin, Nottingham, Sir Edward Banks, Waterloo*
1828—*Ramona*

CHAPTER THREE   OCEAN PIONEERS   (To c 1840)

Page 37   Apart from her first voyage, *Great Western*'s other early sailings were a success and the Great Western Steam Ship Company paid a 9 per cent dividend in 1838. On her own, however, *Great Western* was unable to compete with the Cunard activities and by the time *Great Britain* was available the mail contract opportunity had been lost.

CHAPTER FOUR   COAST AND ESTUARY   (1825–50)

Page 49   London & Blackwall Railway half-yearly reports contain further information regarding the steamer services, viz : 28 February 1842—First steamer *(Eclipse)* arranged for a service to Herne Bay, Margate, Ramsgate, and Dover. 28 February 1843— No dividend : steamboat traffic expanding but not as fast as expected. Fares raised by 2d per passenger. In addition to the fifteen minutes service to Woolwich and Gravesend, all the Star company and the Sons of the Thames company boats and some of the Diamond boats calling at Blackwall. Services available to Antwerp and Rotterdam.

Page 53   The *Norwich Mercury* for 21 June 1945 contains advertisements for the sailings of the Norfolk Steam Packet Company's *Ailsa Craig* from Yarmouth to London on Friday afternoons; fares 10s (50p) and 5s (25p). Also for the sailings of the 'Fast, Splendid and Commodious Boats' *British Queen* and *Emperor* which sailed from Yarmouth and from Foundry Bridge, Norwich at 9am every weekday. Seven days later the same newspaper advertised an excursion to Yarmouth races from Norwich at a fare of 9d.

CHAPTER FIVE   SHORT SEA SERVICES   (1825–50)

Page 57   The *Frolic* joined *Frugal* on the Glasgow–Belfast run in January 1828 implying that the traffic was expanding rapidly.

Page 59   Langtry vessels from the time of the traffic-sharing agreement were *Falcon* (1835), *Reindeer* (1838), *Sea King* (1845), *Blenheim* (1845), and *Whitehaven* (1849); the Dublin company used *Mersey* (1836), *Athlone* (1837), and *Windsor* (1847).

Page 60   Other St George vessels of this period included *Onward* and *Orinoco*.

Page 61   Paddle steamers of the Isle of Man Steam Packet Co :

Vessel	Built	Length/ Gross Tons	Builder
Mona's Isle	1830	116ft/200tons	John Wood & Co
Mona	1832	98ft/150tons	Robert Napier
Queen of the Isle	1834	128ft/350tons	Robert Napier
King Orry	1842	140ft/433tons	J. Winram
Ben-my-Chree	1845	165ft/399tons	Robert Napier
Tynwald	1846	188ft/700tons	Robert Napier

Page 64   GSN paddle steamers of the period :
1831—London Merchant
1834—City of Hamburg, Fame, Perth
1835—John Bull, Britannia, Rapid, Jupiter
1836—Caledonia, William Joliffe, Albion, Monarch, Mountaineer, Dart, Menai, Tourist
1837—Clarence, Countess of Lonsdale, Giraffe, Ocean, Neptune, Leith
1838—Rainbow
1839—Sir William Wallace
1841—Waterwitch, Vivid, Mercury, Wilberforce
1842—Princess Royal, Trident
1843—Venezuela
1844—Little Western, Magician
1845—Triton
1846—Star
1847—Lion
1848—Albion
1849—Seine, Royal Sovereign
1850—Rhine, Tiger, Monarch

CHAPTER SIX   TRANSATLANTIC HEYDAY   (1838–70)

Page 66   A total of £270,800 was subscribed to the British & North American Royal Mail Steam Packet Company. The Burns brothers took 105 shares, MacIver 80, and Cunard 550, each of £100.

Page 72   The fifth Collins Line vessel was the 3,670ton Adriatic.

Page 73   The Galway Line vessels comprised Pacific, Connaught, Hibernia, Anglia, and Columbia.

Page 74   Early Atlantic paddle steamer records :

Year	Vessel	From	To	Days/ Hours/ Minutes	Av. Speed in knots
1838	Great Western	Bristol	New York	15.00.00	8·00
1840	Britannia	Liverpool	Boston	14.08.00	8·19
1840	Acadia	Liverpool	Halifax	11.04.00	9·28
1840	Britannia	Halifax	Liverpool	10.00.00	10·72
1847	Hibernia	Halifax	Liverpool	9.01.30	11·67
1851	Pacific	New York	Liverpool	9.20.26	13·02
1851	Baltic	Liverpool	New York	9.13.00	13·17
1852	Arctic	New York	Liverpool	9.17.15	13·21
1856	Persia	New York	Queenstown	9.01.45	12·54
1863	Scotia	New York	Queenstown	8.03.00	14·01
1864	Scotia	Queenstown	New York	8.04.34	14·66

CHAPTER SEVEN   THE OTHER OCEANS   (1840–70)

Page 77   The original paddle steamers of the Royal Mail Line comprised :
Forth, Clyde, Tweed, Solway (a)—which sailed to the Caribbean end before the contract commenced—Thames, Tay, Dee, Medway, Trent, Avon, Severn, Teviot, Isis (b), Medina (c)
(a) Lost west of Corunna in 1843
(b) Sank off Bermuda in 1842
(c) Wrecked on a coral reef near Turks Island in 1844

Page 77   The new Royal Mail vessels added following the 1850 mail contract comprised Amazon, Orinoco, Parana, Magdalena, and Demerara. The latter was stranded across the Avon in November 1851, abandoned to the underwriters and eventually reconstructed as a sailing vessel.

Page 79   Early paddle steamers of the Pacific Steam Navigation Company :
1845—Ecuador (323tons)
1846—New Grenada (649tons)
1849—Bolivia (773tons)
1850—Santiago (961tons), Lima (1,461tons), Bogota (1,461tons), Quito (1,461tons)
1856—Inca (290tons), Valparaiso (1,060tons)

Page 80   The two bids for the 1837 contract for the Spanish and Portuguese mails were :
Peninsular Steam Navigation Company—£32,684; vessels *Don Juan, Tagus, Braganza, Iberia, Liverpool*
Commercial Steam Navigation Company—£33,750; vessels *Chieftain, Monarch, Emerald, Victoria, William Penn*
The contract commenced 22 August 1837 at £29,600 per annum.

Page 82   Other P&O paddle steamers not mentioned in the main text are listed below :

Construction	Vessel	Gross tonnage	Period
Wood	*Precursor*	1,800tons	1844–58
	India	1,000tons	1845–48
	Lady Mary Wood	550tons	1843–52
Iron	*Ariel*	700tons	1846–48
	Erin	800tons	1846–57
	Pottinger	1,400tons	1846–62
	Haddington	1,650tons	1846–53
	Ripon	1,500tons	1846–70
	Indus	1,400tons	1847–62
	Pekin	1,200tons	1847–67
	Sultan	1,100tons	1847–69
	Euxine	1,150tons	1847–69
	Malta	1,200tons	1848–76
	Achilles	1,000tons	1848–56
	Singapore	1,200tons	1850–67
	Ganges	1,200tons	1850–71

CHAPTER EIGHT   THE SECOND HALF OF THE CENTURY
(1850–1900)

Page 87   The steel paddle steamers obtained by General Steam Navigation from 1887 for the new Yarmouth service were *Halcyon, Mavis, Oriole, Laverock,* and *Philomel.*
Other GSN paddle steamers obtained up to 1900 were :
1851—*Concordia, Panther*
1852—*Ravensbourne, Moselle*
1853—*Edinburgh, Denmark, Holland, Topaz, Hanover, Newcastle, Belgium*
1854—*Ruby, Sapphire*
1855—*Diamond, Dolphin*
1856—*Eagle, Leo*

1858—*Cologne*
1861—*Berlin, Perth*
1862—*Chevy Chase, Sir Walter Raleigh, Waterloo*
1863—*Earl of Aberdeen*
1865—*Orion*
1866—*Eider, Florence, Taurus*
1867—*Hollandia*
1868—*Hilda*
1873—*Hoboken*
1875—*Atlas, Swallow, Swift*
1887—*Halcyon*
1888—*Mavis, Oriole*
1889—*Laverock, Philomel*
1898—*Eagle*

Page 88   Isle of Man Steam Packet Company paddle steamers 1850–1900 :

Vessel	Built	Length/Gross Tons	Builder
Mona's Queen	1852	*186·4ft/600tons	J. & G. Thomson
Douglas	1858	*205ft/700tons	
Mona's Isle (II)	1860	207ft/380tons	Tod & McGregor
Snaefell	1863	*236ft/700tons	Caird & Co
Douglas (II)	1864	*227·4ft/709tons	Caird & Co
Tynwald (II)	1866	*240ft/700tons	Caird & Co
King Orry (II)	1871	298ft/1,104tons	R. Duncan & Co
Ben-my-Chree (II)	1875	318ft/1,192tons	Barrow Ship-building Co
Snaefell (II)	1876	295·5ft/849tons	Caird & Co
Mona's Isle (III)	1882	338ft/1,564tons	Caird & Co
Mona's Queen (II)	1885	328ft/1,559tons	Barrow S Co
Queen Victoria	1887	341·5ft/1,547tons	
Prince of Wales	1887	341·5ft/1,547tons	
Empress Queen	1897	372ft/1,995tons	Fairfield Ship-building & Engineering Co

* Length between perpendiculars

Page 89   After failing to acquire the ex-LNW Holyhead vessels *Munster* and *Leinster* (which spent 1897 in the service of the Isle of Man Steam Packet Company) Liverpool & Douglas Steamers Ltd eventually introduced the ex-LB&SC paddlers *Normandy* and *Brittany*.

Page 90   Of the vessels taken over by the Admiralty in 1837 for the English Channel mail service (see notes for Chapter Ten), *Onyx*, *Violet*, and *Garland* survived to pass to Jenkins & Church-ward in 1854. *Ondine*, which also passed to the new contractors as *Undine*, had been acquired by the Admiralty in 1847. Replacement vessels included *Queen* and *Empress* in 1854, *Prince Frederick William* in 1857, and *John Penn* in 1859.

CHAPTER NINE   THE RÔLE OF THE RAILWAYS   (1840–1900)

Page 95   The early steamers of the South Western Steam Packet Company included :

Vessel	Built	Length/Gross Tons	Builder
Wonder	1844	158ft	Ditchburn & Mare
Transit	1843	267tons	Ditchburn & Mare
Courier	1847	167ft/265tons	Ditchburn & Mare
Dispatch	1847	171ft/288tons	Ditchburn & Mare
Express	1847		Ditchburn & Mare
Alliance	1855	175·5ft/400tons	Ditchburn & Mare
Havre	1856	184·7ft/225tons	Ditchburn & Mare
Southampton	1860	215·5ft/585tons	Palmer Bros & Co

Page 96   South Eastern & Continental Steam Packet Company paddle steamers :

Vessel	Built	Length/Gross Tons	Builder
Princess Maud	1844	140·5ft/177tons	Ditchburn & Mare
Princess Mary	1844	294tons	Ditchburn & Mare
Queen of the Belgians	1844	164ft/207tons	Ditchburn & Mare
Queen of the French	1845	207tons	Ditchburn & Mare
Prince Ernest	1845	183·1ft/272tons	Laird, Birkenhead
Princess Helena	1846	166·2ft/267tons	Laird, Birkenhead
Princess Clementine	1846	165·3ft/252tons	Laird, Birkenhead
Lord Warden	1847	168ft/307tons	Laird, Birkenhead

Page 97   The vessels operated under an arrangement between the London, Chatham & Dover Railway and Jenkins & Churchward from 1862 to 1864 included *Garland, Queen, Empress, Prince Frederick William, John Penn, Jupiter, Scout, Pathfinder, Pioneer, Poet, Samphire, Maid of Kent, Etoile du Nord*, and *Undine*.

Page 99   Portsmouth–Isle of Wight paddle steamers of the LB&SC and L&SW railways :

Vessel	Built	Length/ Gross Tons	Builder
Victoria	1881	191·9ft/366tons	Aitken & Mansel
Duchess of Edinburgh	1884	190·6ft/342tons	Aitken & Mansel
Duchess of Connaught	1884	190·6ft/342tons	Aitken & Mansel
Duchess of Albany	1889	170·4ft/256tons	Scott & Co
Princess Margaret	1893	170·6ft/260tons	Scott & Co
Duchess of Kent	1897	195·4ft/399tons	Day, Summers & Co
Duchess of Fife	1899	215ft/443tons	Clydebank E&SB Co
Duchess of Richmond	1910	190·2ft/354tons	D. & W. Henderson & Co
Duchess of Norfolk	1911	190ft/381tons	D. & W. Henderson & Co

Page 100   Vessels working the 1863 LNW freight service between Holyhead and Dublin :

Vessel	Built	Length/Gross Tons	Builder
Alexandra	1863	226·6ft/703tons	Lairds
Stanley	1864	239·2ft/782tons	Caird & Co
Sea Nymph	1845	206·3ft/685tons	Caird & Co
Admiral Moorsom	1860	219·3ft/794tons	Elder & Co
Telegraph	1853	244·0ft/848tons	J. & G. Thomson

Page 100   Barrow Steam Navigation Company vessels :

Vessel	Built	Length/ Gross Tons	Builder
Roe	1864	236·6ft/559tons	Caird & Co
Talbot/Armagh	1860	263·5ft/631tons	D. & W. Henderson & Co
Shelburne/Tyrone	1860	269·6ft/616tons	D. & W. Henderson & Co
Herald	1866	221·6ft/446tons	Caird & Co
Antrim/Manxman	1870	266·6ft/797tons	R. Duncan & Co
Londonderry	1866	243·2ft/701tons	Caird & Co
Donegal	1865	241·1ft/689tons	Caird & Co
Duchess of Edinburgh/Manx Queen	1881	278·9ft/969tons	J. & G. Thomson
Duchess of Buccleugh	1888	250·6ft/838tons	Fairfield S&E Co

Page 101   The steamers taken over by the Lancashire & Yorkshire Railway from the Drogheda Steam Packet Company were *Tredagh, Nora Creina, Kathleen Mavoureen,* and *Iverna.*

Page 101   Principal GWR paddle steamers were *Vulture, Great Western, South of Ireland, Malakhoff, Limerick, Milford, Limerick* (II), *Waterford,* and *Pembroke.*

Page 102   Principal GER paddle steamers were *Zealous, Harwich,*

Avalon, Richard Young, Pacific, Claud Hamilton, Princess of Wales, Lady Tyler, and *Adelaide.*

CHAPTER TEN   THE ROYAL NAVY   (1820–1970)

Page 110   The vessels taken over by the Admiralty from the Post Office with the English Channel mail services in 1837 and subsequent vessels used thereon included :

Vessel	Built	Tonnage	Builder
Ariel	1826	150	Ex Post Office *Arrow,* refitted Woolwich 1837
Widgeon	1837	225	Chatham Royal Dockyard
Dover	1840	224	Laird Bros
Princess Alice	1843	270	Ditchburn & Mare. Bought 1844. Refitted Woolwich
Onyx	1845	292	Ditchburn & Mare
Violet	1845	292	Ditchburn & Mare
Scout	1845	111	Ditchburn & Mare
Garland	1846	292	Fletcher of Limehouse
Vivid	1848	352	Chatham Royal Dockyard
Jupiter	1850	280	Miller & Ravenhill

Page 110   Commissioned in 1832, PS *Rhadamanthus* was the first steam vessel to be built at Devonport and the first Navy steamer to cross the Atlantic. Of 813tons, she was 190ft long and had 20nhp side-lever engines by Maudslay, Sons & Field. She lasted until 1864 undertaking blockade work off the Dutch coast and then survey and local work in the West Indies.

Page 113   The Ascot class of paddle minesweepers was made up of the following vessels :

Lost—*Ascot* (November 1918), *Kempton* and *Redcar* (June 1917), *Ludlow* (December 1916), *and Plumpton* (October 1918)

Broken Up—*Totnes* (mined December 1916 but repaired), *Chelmsford, Cheltenham, Chepstow, Croxton, Doncaster, Eglington, Epsom, Eridge, Gatwick, Goodwood, Haldon, Hurst, Lingfield, Newbury, Pontefract, Sandown,* and 1918 vessels *Shirley, Banbury, Hexham, Lanark, Wetherby, Lewes, Harpenden,* and *Shincliffe.*

Sold—*Atherstone*—renamed *Queen of Kent* and *Melton*—renamed *Queen of Thanet*

Page 115　The Director class of diesel-electric paddle tugs embraced HM vessels *Director, Forceful, Grinder, Griper, Faithful, Favourite,* and *Dexterous.*

CHAPTER ELEVEN　UNUSUAL AND NOTABLE VESSELS　(1815–1970)

Page 120　The 'Eagles' of the General Steam Navigation Company :

Vessel	Built	Length/ Gross Tons	Builder
Eagle	1824	125ft/56tons net	
Eagle	1856	200ft/325tons	At Northfleet
Eagle	1898	265ft/647tons	Gourlay Brothers
Golden Eagle	1909	275·7ft/793tons	John Brown & Co
Crested Eagle	1925	299·7ft/1,110tons	J. Samuel White & Co
Royal Eagle	1932	289·75ft/1,538tons	Cammell Laird & Co

CHAPTER TWELVE　PADDLE STEAMER INCIDENTS

In addition to the better known and particularly dramatic incidents recorded in this chapter, the other chapters will have made it clear that quite a large number of paddle steamers did not survive to retire as hulks or to scrapyards. Some, like the *Maid of Lorn,* sank more than once (in the Crinan Canal) while others seemed to make collisions a speciality, eg, the Mersey ferry PS *Wirral.* The combination of a great deal of wood in the construction, coal-fired furnaces and smokers among the passengers meant that fires were not infrequent and *Grenadier, Gairlochy,* and *Vesta* provide examples from the Clyde area. Despite the number of incidents, the serious casualties were very small indeed in relation to the total amount of activity—a tribute to the fine body of seamen who manned the paddle steamers. The casualties that did occur were mainly in the relatively crowded waters of the main estuaries of the Thames, the Mersey, and the Clyde. Both the Humber and the Solent seem to have a somewhat better record, possibly because the competitive element was less as well as the overall amount of activity.

CHAPTER THIRTEEN　DESIGN, CONSTRUCTION, AND MACHINERY

Engines

Side-Lever—usually installed in pairs; comprised cylinder, piston rod and side rods on one end of the side levers and cross tail and connecting rod on the other. Since each side lever was pivoted, the piston raising one end must lower the connecting rod at the other.

Steeple—vertical cylinder with piston rod above and twin connecting rods working directly onto the crank pins for each wheel shaft.

Grasshopper—virtually a beam engine with the cylinder between the gudgeon and the connecting rod.

Oscillating—piston rods acting directly onto the crank by the device of pivoting the cylinders.

Boilers

Flue—cylindrical shell containing one furnace tube fed by a long grate. Exhaust gases returned by external tube to the front of the boiler and thence to the funnel

Rectangular—gases from the furnace via the combustion chamber through numerous firetubes stretching from the rear of the furnace to smokeboxes above the doors. These boilers were usually installed so that the firemen and coaltrimmers and also the exhaust uptakes came together at the centre line of the vessel.

Cylindrical (Scotch)—a development of the rectangular boiler eliminating a large amount of the weight of stays.

Haystack—virtually a vertical Scotch boiler with increased diameter and reduced height.

Gunboat—early application of locomotive type of furnace/boiler combination; used for light, fast vessels.

Wheels

Radial—fixed form of paddle wheel used on the earlier vessels and on the high seas where feathering paddles would not have been sufficiently robust.

Feathering—variable angle paddle blades moved by eccentrics so as to emerge from the water at a fine angle and thus not retard the forward motion of the vessel.

Condensers

Jet—exhaust steam condensed by being mixed with a jet of cold water.

Surface—cooling water passed through the exhaust steam in tubes.
  Cylinders decreased in size (bore and stroke) as steam pressures increased.

N

CHAPTER FOURTEEN
FERRY, TUG, AND OTHER SPECIAL-PURPOSE VESSELS

Page 148   The scrapping of *Houghton* in 1964 left at work only
the commercial paddle tugs *Roker* at Methil, *Reliant* at Seaham,
Eppleton Hall at Sunderland, and *John H Amos* at Middlesbrough :

Vessel	Built	Length/ Gross Tons	Builder
Houghton	1904	101ft/133tons	W. Hepple & Co
Roker		100ft	Rennoldson
Reliant	1907	100ft/156tons	J. T. Eltringham & Co
Eppleton Hall	1914	105ft/166tons	W. Hepple & Co
John H Amos	1931	110ft/202tons	Bow McLachlan & Co Ltd

CHAPTER FIFTEEN   EXCURSION HEYDAY   (1850–1939)

Page 158   The original vessels of the Southampton, Isle of Wight
& South of England Steam Packet Company Ltd were *Ruby*
(110tons), *Pearl* (48tons), *Queen* (95tons), *Medina* (145tons), *Gem*
(138tons), *Emerald* (100tons), and *Sapphire* with *Lord of the Isles*
(104tons) and *Lady of the Lake* (126tons), being acquired in 1865.

Page 159   At the time of their Southampton challenge P. & A.
Campbell operated the following vessels :

Vessel	Built	Length/Gross Tons	Builder
Waverley	1885	205ft/258tons	H. McIntyre & Co
Ravenswood	1891	215ft/391tons	S. McKnight & Co
Westward Ho	1894	225ft/438tons	S. McKnight & Co
Cambria	1895	225ft/420tons	H. McIntyre & Co
Britannia	1896	230ft/459tons	S. McKnight & Co
Lady Margaret	1895	210ft/369tons	A. McMillan & Son
Glen Rosa	1877	206ft/223tons	Caird & Co

Page 159   South coast paddle steamers in 1910 :

Hastings, St Leonards & Eastbourne Steamboat Co Ltd—*Glen
Rosa, Britannia, Cynthia*

R. R. Collard, Newhaven—*May, Lynton, Plymouth Belle,
Southampton*

Weymouth, Bournemouth & Swanage Steam Packets Ltd—
*Empress, Queen, Victoria, Monarch, Albert Victor, Majestic,
Emperor of India*

Port of Portsmouth & Ryde United Steam Packet Co—*Alexandra*

Joint Railways—*Duchess of Edinburgh, Duchess of Connaught, Duchess of Albany, Princess Margaret, Duchess* of *Kent, Duchess of Fife, Duchess of Richmond*

L&SWR—*Lymington, Solent* (III)

Southampton, Isle of Wight & South of England Royal Mail Steam Packet Co Ltd—*Solent Queen, Prince of Wales, Duchess of York, Lorna Doone, Balmoral, Queen* (II), *Stirling Castle, Bournemouth Queen, Lord Elgin*

Other operators—*Worthing Belle, Bembridge, Premier, Duke of Devonshire, Duchess of Devonshire, Empress, Princess Royal, Alexandra*

Page 159 Population figures for Eastbourne exemplify the growth of the south coast resorts :

1801	1,668
1881	21,510
1921	62,028
1967	66,800

Page 160 For new GSN vessels 1887 to 1889 see notes for Chapter Eight.

Page 160 'Belle' steamers of the London, Woolwich & Clacton-on-Sea Steamboat Company/Belle Steamers Ltd/Coast Development Corporation Ltd :

Vessel	Built	Length/Gross Tons	Builder
Clacton Belle	1890	246ft/458tons	Wm. Denny & Bros
Woolwich Belle	1891	200ft/298tons	Wm. Denny & Bros
London Belle	1893	280ft/738tons	Wm. Denny & Bros
Southend Belle	1896	249ft/570tons	Wm. Denny & Bros
Walton Belle	1897	230ft/465tons	Wm. Denny & Bros
Yarmouth Belle	1898	240ft/522tons	Wm. Denny & Bros
Southwold Belle	1900	245·3ft/535tons	Wm. Denny & Bros

Page 162 New Medway Steam Packet Company vessels :

Vessel	Built	Length/Gross Tons	Builder
Princess of Wales	1896	139·6ft/163tons	R. Craggs & Sons
Audrey	1897	126ft/203tons	Armstrong Whitworth & Co

Queen of the South—ex *Woolwich Belle* ⎫
Essex Queen—ex *Walton Belle* ⎬ see above
Queen of Southend—ex *Yarmouth Belle* ⎭

Vessel	Built	Length/Gross Tons	Builder
Queen of Kent—ex HMS Atherstone			Ailsa Shipbuilding Co
Queen of Thanet—ex HMS Melton			W. Hamilton & Co
Medway Queen	1924	179·9ft	Ailsa Shipbuilding Co
City of Rochester	1904	160·2ft	J. Scott & Co
Clacton Queen	1897	195·4ft/399tons	Day, Summers & Co

Page 164   Paddle steamers of the Liverpool & North Wales Steamship Company Ltd in the twentieth century :

Vessel	Built	Length/Gross Tons	Builder
Bonnie Princess	1882	240ft/434tons	T. B. Seath & Co
St Tudno	1889	265·2ft/987tons	Fairfield SB&E Co
St Tudno (II)	1891	265·4ft/994tons	Fairfield SB&E Co
St Elvies	1896	240·6ft/567tons	Fairfield SB&E Co
Snowdon (II)	1892	175ft/338tons	Fairfield SB&E Co
La Marguerite	1894	330ft/2,205tons	Fairfield SB&E Co
St. Elian (I)	1872	150·1ft/203tons	Barclay, Curle & Co
St Trillo (I)	1876	165·7ft/198tons	Barclay, Curle & Co

CHAPTER SIXTEEN   PADDLERS AT WAR

Page 167   Other blockade runners included *Alice* (635tons), *Fannie* (635tons)—both from Cairds—*Dawn* (705tons), the 552ton *Fergus* and *The Dare* from Stephens, the ex-MacBrayne *Dolphin* and *Mail* (158·7tons) from Tod & McGregor.

World War I:

Page 169   GSN vessels lost—*Halcyon* (553tons), *Oriole* (387tons), and *Philomel* (564tons).

Page 169   Isle of Man Steam Packet Co :

Vessel	Built	Length/Gross Tons	
Prince of Wales			
(Prince Edward)	1887	341·5ft/1,547tons	Sold Admiralty
Queen Victoria	1887	341·5ft/1,547tons	Sold Admiralty
Mona's Isle (III)	1882	338ft/1,564tons	Sold Admiralty
Empress Queen	1897	372ft/1,995tons	Foundered Feb 1916
Mona's Queen (II)	1885	328ft/1,559tons	Resumed peacetime service until 1929

World War II:

Page 175   On Friday 1 September 1939 the GSN fleet was deployed to evacuate children from London as follows :

To Yarmouth—PS *Golden Eagle,* MV *Queen of the Channel*
To Lowestoft—PS *Royal Eagle,* MV *Royal Daffodil*
To Felixstowe—MV *Crested Eagle,* PS *Medway Queen,* PS *Thames Queen*
Royal Sovereign was also used on this work and accompanied the others (with *Queen of Thanet* in place of *Thames Queen*) to Dunkirk.

Page 176   South Coast paddle steamer victims :

Vessel	Built	Length/ Gross Tons	Builder	
Devonia	1905	245ft/ 641tons	P. & A. Campbell	Beached Dunkirk
Barry/Waverley	1907	225·6ft/ 471tons	P. & A. Campbell	1941
Glen Avon	1912	220ft/ 509tons	P. & A. Campbell	1944
Brighton Belle	1900	200ft/ 320tons	P. & A. Campbell	Dunkirk 1940
Brighton Queen	1905	245ft/ 519tons	P. & A. Campbell	Dunkirk 1940
Portsdown	1928	190ft/ 342tons	Southern Railway	Mined 1941
Southsea (II)	1930	244ft/ 825tons	Southern Railway	Mined 1941
Gracie Fields	1936	195·9ft/ 393tons	Southampton company	Dunkirk 1940

CHAPTER SEVENTEEN   THE TWENTIETH CENTURY   (1900–1939)

Page 180   *Prince George* and *Princess Mary* were built in 1898 by A. & J. Inglis for the use of the North British Steam Packet Company on Loch Lomond. The vessels were similar, 170ft long and of 256tons. *Prince George* worked the Balloch–Ardlui service with *Princess Mary* acting as spare and weekend boat. The former lasted until 1942, the latter until 1952.

Page 185   The new SR vessels were as follows :

Shanklin	1924	Replaced *Duchess of Richmond*
Freshwater	1927	Lymington–Yarmouth
Portsdown	1928	Replaced *Duchess of Albany*
Merstone	1928	Replaced *Princess Margaret*

N*

Southsea	1930	Excursion work
Whippingham	1930	Excursion work
Sandown	1934	Replaced *Duchess of Kent*
Ryde	1937	

MacBrayne paddle steamers in the twentieth century :

Displaced

1902—*Islay* (III)	Tod & McGregor (1872)
1904—*Lovedale*	W. Simons & Co (1867)
1904—*Countess of Kellie*	A. Stephen & Son (1870)
1905—*Glendale*	J. Elder & Co (1875)
1909—*Mountaineer* (II)	T. Wingate & Co (1858)
1909—*Carabinier*	Oswald, Mordaunt & Co (1878)
1912—*Lochness*	J. Barr (1853)
1919—*Gairlochy*	Barclay, Curle & Co (1861)
1925—*Gael*	Robertson & Co (1867)
1927—*Chevalier* (II)	J. & G. Thomson (1866)
1928—*Grenadier*	J. & G. Thomson (1885)
1936—*Columba*	J. & G. Thomson (1878)
1936—*Iona* (III)	J. & G. Thomson (1864)
1939—*Gondolier*	J. & G. Thomson (1866)

CHAPTER EIGHTEEN   DECLINE AND PRESERVATIOON   (1945–70)

Page 189   Clyde cruise/excursion picture in 1962 :

Waverley	Mondays	Brodick and Whiting Bay outwards via Kyles of Bute, return via Garroch Head
Jeanie Deans	Mon-Fri	Cruise round Bute, outward via Garroch Head
Waverley	Tues, Thurs and Sats	Lochgoilhead and Arrochar
Waverley	Wednesdays	Round the Lochs
Waverley	Fridays	Evening 'Circle' cruises to Dunoon and Largs
Waverley or *Jeanie Deans*	Selected Sundays	(1) Round Bute, outwards via Largs Channel (2) Skipness (Kintyre)
Waverley	Sundays	Kyles of Bute

Talisman	Sundays	Tighnabruaich and Kyles of Bute
Talisman	Mon-Fri	Cumbrae circle cruises (from Largs, Rothesay and Millport)
Jeanie Deans	Saturdays	Tighnabruaich and Kyles of Bute
Caledonia	Thursdays	Ayr and Troon to Brodick (Arran), Rothesay and Dunoon
Caledonia	Sundays	Dunoon, Loch Goil; Rothesay, Loch Riddon
	Mondays	Whiting Bay; Rothesay; Campbeltown
	Tuesdays	Millport, Dunoon and Loch Goil; Rothesay and Tighnabruaich
	Wednesdays	Brodick, Whiting Bay and Millport

Throughout this book references to the tonnage of vessels is normally to the gross tonnage based on the enclosed vessel capacity reckoned at 100 cubic feet to the ton. In the case of early vessels capacity was expressed in terms of wine 'tuns', ie, 42cu ft to the ton. References to length are to overall length rather than length between perpendiculars and to the Clyde cover both the Firth and the western islands.

ACKNOWLEDGEMENTS

ANY book normally owes much to people other than the author; to the wife, the friends, the publisher and his staff; to the individuals who help so generously with information, and to the many official bodies whose records contribute so much. I am deeply indebted to all these people and, in particular, to—

Mrs Edith Cooil BM, MM; Messrs R. J. Franklin, W. S. Hoare, W. R. G. Hopkins, A. P. Shimmin, C. R. Temple, P. Thomas, and F. M. Walker.

C. W. Black Esq MA, FLA, City Librarian, Corporation of Glasgow; A. S. E. Browning Esq, Glasgow Museum and Art Galleries; W. Brundan Esq, OBE, DL, MEng, CEng, County Engineer and Surveyor, Pembrokeshire County Council; City of Southampton, Museums Department; Coast Lines Ltd; Corporation of London, Guildhall Library; Dartmouth Borough Museum; David MacBrayne Ltd; Devon Dock, Pier & Steamship Co Ltd; Durham County Library; *Eastern Evening News*; Paul W. Elkin Esq, Curator of Technology, City Museum, Bristol; General Post Office; General Steam Navigation Company; Greater London Council; A. A. C. Hedges Esq, FLA, Borough Librarian & Curator, Great Yarmouth Public Libraries & Museums; Imperial War Museum; Isle of Man Steam Packet Company; Isle of Man Tourist Board; *Isle of Man Weekly Times*; P. Lamb Esq, Curator, Paddle Steamer Preservation Society; Graham Large Esq, *Fish Trades Gazette*; Ministry of Defence (Navy); National Maritime Museum; D. W. Patterson Esq, Purdy Trawlers Ltd; Peninsular & Oriental Steam Navigation Company; Port of London Authority; River Dart Steamboat Co Ltd; Scarborough Public Libraries, Museums and Art Galleries; Science Museum, South Kensington; John H. Scholes Esq, Curator of Historic Relics, British Railways Board; Seaham Harbour Dock Company; M. K. Stammers Esq, Keeper of Shipping, City of Liverpool Museums; Upper Clyde Shipbuilders Ltd.

BIBLIOGRAPHY

I n preparing a book with as broad a scope as this one, reference must needs be made to a vast range of material. Many unlikely sources add to the available information on the subject while a variety of different works have contributed to the background material, including the old Baddeley & Ward 'Thorough Guides' series. Other sources of local material have been county magazines and local newspapers as well as the many individuals acknowledged elsewhere. To mention all the references would be impossible. East Anglia alone involves the *Norwich Mercury*, the *Eastern Evening News, East Anglian Magazine*, and *Essex Countryside* while further data appear in national journals like the *Fish Trades Gazette* and *Paddle Wheels*, the magazine of the Paddle Steamer Preservation Society.

Among the books containing paddle steamer references are :

Armstrong, Warren. *Atlantic Highway*
Atthill, Robin. *The Somerset & Dorset Railway*
Barker, T. C. and Robbins, Michael. *A History of London Transport*
Bowen. *A century of Atlantic Travel*
Bucknall, Rixon. *Boat Trains and Channel Packets*
Burtt, F. *Cross Channel and Coastal Paddle Steamers, Steamers of the Thames and Medway*
Clegg, W. Paul and Styring, John S. *Steamers of British Railways and Associated Companies*
Duckworth, C. L. D. and Langmuir, G. E. *West Highland Steamers, Railway and Other Steamers, West Coast Steamers, Clyde River and Other Steamers*
Farr, Grahame. *West Country Passenger Steamers*
Fletcher, R. A. *Steam-ships*
Gibbs, Commander C. R. Vernon. *British Passenger Liners of the Five Oceans*
Graseman, C. and McLachlan G. W. P. *English Channel Packet Boats*

Grimshaw, G. *British Pleasure Steamers 1920–1939*
Hambleton, F. C. *Famous Paddle Steamers*
Harnack, Edwin P. *All About Ships and Shipping*
Herbert, A. P. *The Thames*
Holmes, Sir George C. V. *Ancient and Modern Ships*
Jackman, W. T. *The Development of Transportation in Modern England*
Kennedy, John. *The History of Steam Navigation*
Laird Clowes, Wm. *The Royal Navy*
Le Fleming, H. M. *Warships of World War I*
Lewis, Michael. *The Navy of Britain*
Lindsay, W. S. *History of Merchant Shipping 1816–1874*
McQueen, A. *Clyde River Steamers of the Last Fifty Years, Echoes of Old Clyde Paddle Wheels*
Maginnis. *The Atlantic Ferry*
Nock, O. S. *The Caledonian Railway*
Pannell, J. P. M. *Old Southampton Shores*
Parker, Captain H. and Bowen, Frank C. *Mail and Passenger Steamships of the 19th Century*
Reader, Ernest R. *Linking Belfast and Liverpool*
Robinson, Howard. *Carrying British Mails Overseas*
Sherington, C. E. R. *A Hundred Years of Inland Transport*
Spratt, H. Philip. *The Birth of the Steamboat: Transatlantic Paddle Steamers*
Thornley, F. C. *Steamers of North Wales*
Thornton, E. C. B. *South Coast Pleasure Steamers*
Williamson, Capt John. *Clyde Passenger Steamers*
Willson, Beckles. *The Story of Rapid Transit Coastwise Trade of the United Kingdom, George Thompson, The Centenary of the Isle of Man Steam Packet Co Ltd*

Handbooks of the Belfast Transport Museum, Sea Breezes, Ships Illustrated, Ships Monthly, various railway histories and steamer company handbooks

INDEX

Illustrations are indicated by italic figures

221

230 INDEX

Tyne Steamboat, 146
Tynwald, 61, 89, 201, 204
Tyrone, 206

Ulster, 99
Uncle Sam, 94
Undine, 90, 94, 127, 205
Unicorn, 66
Union, 152
United Service, 147
Unusual vessels, 18, 28, 29, 35,
116–118, 152

Valetta, 82
Valparaiso, 79, 202
Vectis, 82
Velocity, 45
Venezuela, 201
Venus, 49, 168, 199
Vernon, 116
Vesta, 53, 208
Victoria, 45–46, 97, 99, 203, 206,
210
Victory, 29, 60, 199
Violet, 90, 100, 205, 207
Vista, 105
Vivid, 45, 201, 207
Vulcan, 136, 176
Vulture, 206

Walton Belle, 172, 211
Warrior, 93, 136
War activities, 19, 68, 113–114,
123–124, 166–176, 212–213
Warships, 19, 35, 67, 110–114, 207
Waterford, 206, *103*
Waterloo, 27, 55, 199, 204
Waterman, 49
Waterwitch, 201
Watt, James, 16, 18, 19, 20, 120,
133, 134

Waverley, 163, 171, 175, 188, 195,
210, 213, 214
Wemyss Bay Railway, 94, 106, 130
Westonia, 154, 157
Westward Ho, 160, 182, 187, 210
Wetherby, 207
Weymouth, 91, 101, 124, 157, 190
Whippingham, 189, 214
Whitehaven, 200
Widgeon, 207
Wilberforce, 201
Will Crooks, 152
William Fawcett, 80
William Joliffe, 201
William Penn, 203
William the Fourth, 60
William Wallace, 96
Windsor, 200
Wingfield Castle, 196
Wirral, 208
Wolf, 94
Wonder, 205
Wood, John, shipbuilder, 20, 21, 22,
24, 60, 61, 69, 201
Woolwich, 46, 47, 48, 49, 93, 109,
110, 151, 161, 180, 200, 207
Woolwich Belle, 159, 160, 211
Woolwich Free Ferry, 132, 151–152,
175–176, 189
Woolwich Steam Packet Co, 47, 48,
49, 93
Worthing Belle, 211

Yarmouth Belle, 211
Yarmouth (Great), 30, 53, 87, 147,
157, 160, 180, 184, 199, 200, 203,
213

Zealous, 102, 206